GRAIL

An Essay on the Mystery of Sacred Love

This edition is a translation of *Graal: Saggio sul Mistero del Sacro Amore* by Massimo Scaligero, originally published by Perseo, Rome, 1969. Reprinted by Tilopa, Rome, 2001.

Published with the support of the Fern Hill Fund

ISBN: 979-8-9874429-7-5

First English edition

Translation copyright 2025 © Eric L. Bisbocci

Publication made possible through the collaboration with Associazione Culturale Fondazione Massimo Scaligero
Published in 2025
By Alkion Press
330 Route 21, Ghent, NY 12075

Title: *Grail: An Essay on the Mystery of Sacred Love*

Author: Massimo Scaligero
Translation: Eric L. Bisbocci
Layout and Design: Ella Manor Lapointe.
Cover Concept: Eric G. Müller

The cover combines Photos of *Even Song* by Agnes Pelton and *Susanna and the Elders* by Massimo Stanzione (Städel Museum, Frankfurt, Germany).

Thank you to the Agnes Pelton Society.

Massimo Scaligero

GRAIL

An Essay on the Mystery of Sacred Love

Translated by
Eric L. Bisbocci

ALKION
PRESS

The translation of this text is dedicated to the Bianchi family in Rome, who throughout the years graciously took me into their home and in 1979 introduced me to the writings of Rudolf Steiner and Massimo Scaligero. From then on, my life forever changed.

To Marina Sagramora

CONTENTS

1.

THE ADAMANTINE PATH OF THE WEST

There, where further descent is impossible, for lack of an original substance to further degrade, it may happen that one attempts to spiritualize the degree of the fall, according to a value that is conceivable at that level. And so, the task of reintegrating that which is dead is proposed, namely a vitalization of the corpse. Thus sex, having fallen into a general automatism (which is its abstractness filled with instinctive *hubris*), comes today to have its own esotericism, not because it can have an esoteric counterpart under similar conditions, but because, at that level, any doctrine can bend to justify its content.

In fact, today, at the level where we are, doctrines to reintegrate the subhuman, which has become an existential condition, cannot exist, but only operational techniques of consciousness on itself. This is understandable, if we admit that, whatever the degree of abjection achieved, this (degree), however, is possible to the extent that there is a consciousness that identifies with it or supports it.

On the plane where the inner operation separating the idea of sex from that of love is no longer possible, so that the mythologizing of sex is indistinguishable from love as a metaphysical principle, any method of reintegration lacking the means to perceive the massive impediment opposed to it—made up of the present-day dialectical condition of consciousness—is destined to fuel misunderstanding. Which is the last-ditch effort of the subhuman: its own spiritual dignification. Unable to escape such a condition is Tantrism, the doctrinaire system that, placing Shakti or the original cosmic power at the center, recognizes in sex the human function where Shakti is more deeply hidden and can be reawakened. Which thought nevertheless is capable of thinking Shakti? What we regard as power presupposes a knowing of its own, which, unpossessed as a value, cannot but be a relative measure of power. Undoubtedly, the tantric system, where the [various] metaphysics of India converge and permeate one another (from the ancient Vedic ritualism to the recent Visnuito mysticism[1]), bears a new element into the world of the Tradition, namely an awareness of the changed inner constitution of the human being of *Kali Yuga* and the demand for a new type of a metaphysical action. However, *it cannot know such a need with respect to the human being of the technological age.*

The stability of Tantrism wields a particular fascination over today's weakened human being, who longs for the magical force. Tantric texts seem to possess the knowledge that lies at the heart of modern philosophy in the West, regarding the exhausted function of ancient metaphysics. Help from the gods, from revelations, from inspirations is no longer given. The gods abandoned us so that we could sustain ourselves and realize, through our own power, the original nature within us. Those who wish to turn back pursue the "path of the dead," since they do nothing but dig up ancient states of consciousness within themselves, beyond which we must move today in order to be. In fact, the gods expect us to pursue the path of freedom to the very end, not our return to a state of dependence that was justified only in ancient times, when we still drew our forces from the womb of the Mother. Over time, the individuality of the human being, accompanied by the correlated revelation, becomes ever more independent of the ancient cosmic matrix, but it pays for this independence through the loss of transcendent states of consciousness. Its experience becomes ever more terrestrial. It is *Kali Yuga*, the dark night that precedes the dawn. The Mother leaves us in the solitude of sensory experience so that we can confront the challenge of freedom. But precisely for this reason, here within matter, within the sensory (realm), within the physical body, the power of the Mother must now be discovered. The decision to discover it cannot be a gift from the Mother, but rather, an autonomous human initiative, namely what we can will, but also not will. The path of freedom is also the path of discovering the Divine, according to a communion incomprehensible to whoever is immersed in that traditionalism

where the Tradition has ceased to flow. To discover the Mother, as
an original virtue, or as the cosmic consciousness with respect to
which modern consciousness is immersed in profound sleep, is
a task whose similar aspects one can recognize in the mysticism
of the West. In Tantrism, the Mother becomes the bride, the
cooperator in the enterprise of reintegration. According to
satchakra sâdhanâ[2], the pure principle of consciousness must be
attained at its location, *sahasrarachakra*[3], from which it draws
the strength to descend to *mûlâdhârachakra*[4] and encounter the
principle of the creative force, Shakti, that sleeps there in the
form of the serpent, *Kundalini.*

The method for realizing such a task, theoretically has some
affinity with the Western idealistic position of *total immanence.*
Each transcendence is an abstraction for those who no longer
perceive the Divine directly; the consciousness from which they
move is the self-identical immediacy, which cannot be ignored
or passed over. The consciousness that one has, the constitution
that one has, the body that one has, are points of departure.
It is a matter of seeing if it is possible to arrive at the radical
nature of these ways of being. If the Divine is at the heart of
the world, it will be discovered. This (is the) assumption that
a "Western" method could theoretically share with the tantric
method—a method that develops according to acts that exclude
every gnoseological presumption, since they are sufficient
unto themselves, as expressions of communion with the primal
power. *Being*, as an outer reality, physical or super-physical, is
opposed to *thinking*, insofar as it is weak thinking that contrasts
it as alterity, or insofar as thinking, by not possessing the act by
means of which it consecrates being, lives as an abstract function,
estranged from its own central power. The reality of being does
not proceed from a principle that can be referred to it but, rather,
from a type of relationship by which the "I" can assume it. What
in Tantrism distinguishes the various forms of experience that
result from it, is the potential of the masculine metaphysical
element's encounter with that of the feminine, according to the
degree at which it is realized.

It is evident that the principle of the dyad, as an immanent
element from which it is inevitable to move, is the essential
point, as a point of departure. What is it? Tantrism cannot

account for such a point of departure, given that it presupposes it. Instead, what can account for it is a Spiritual Science that, gnoseologically, gives an account of absolute immanence and of synthesis as an original act. Tantrism puts aside the intellectual or devotional methods of previous schools, in view of conquering the deepest center of intellectuality and, therefore, of directly controlling life and physical reality. The outer order of things is itself power, but the power of a thing recognized intellectually is a dependency. *Mâyâ* is a way for Shakti to present itself, a power that dominates us, if we are unable to control it. It is *Mâyâshakti*[5]. *Jîvas*[6] can also abandon themselves to the conception of the world as an illusory game, dream, semblance, but this semblance will always have the strength to impose itself on them as a brutal necessity, if its position is merely mental. The fact that Tantrism calls for the certainty of principles to a personal realization— insofar as the power realized is proof of itself—has persuaded more than one scholar that it provides today's human being with an urgent technique, namely that of overcoming the mental limit. However, no account is taken of the fact that Tantrism is incapable of knowing the mental (sphere) of this time.

Pure divine power, the Mother, is realized at each level of manifestation until it assumes for us the guise of *mâyâ*. But, at each level, given that knowledge is one with the act, only the knowing that is able to experience a synthesis at the level of *mâyâ* can account for a level above this. One can grant the ascetics of past Tantrism their yogic experience, but not the possession of the mental element inherent within the technological and logical-mathematical experience. The truly fundamental event is for the ideal of absolute immanence to be realized precisely by such a Western experience. Therefore, the conscious counterpart of this cannot come from other systems, but only from an internal elaboration of its own process, by means of the forces engaged in it. Immanence can become an experience of consciousness, as well as a rationalistic-technological achievement. But it is an event that cannot be realized by means of a *yoga*, even a bold one like that of Tantra.

The world's scenario appears fixed and objective, insofar as one sees it complete in itself, independently of the act of seeing it and of knowing it. However, it is about discovering that we are not only spectators, but actors of such a spectacle. This spectacle lies before us, as a sum of sensory perceptions, continuously transmuting. To see it organically—not as a mere multiplicity of outer notes, but as a harmonious ensemble of elements and minerals, or plants or animals with a human vertex—is an act of the spirit. A formative process of consciousness that leads us to freedom arises from the awareness and from the experience of this direct activity of the spirit. We can begin to free ourselves within the current inside us if we manage to reach the point where its *actualization* as consciousness and the *'self-giving of being'* coincide. The synthesis that we thereby experience is truly the process of world power; *here, the original unity is found.*

Western thinking, to the degree in which it can thereby penetrate reality, bears an element of immanence that Tantrism lacks. The absence of such an element renders the magic-erotic aspect of tantric yoga ambiguous to the modern investigator. *Eros,* in fact, is an inner phenomenon connected to the group of instincts and sensations most irreducible to the domain of knowledge. To make a Shaktic power of *eros* requires the implementation of an original element of consciousness immanent to knowing—namely, to the vehicle of the "I"—and that simultaneously moves in the same current of *kundalini*.

Today, it is about having the capacity, or the courage, to understand that thought, pure in itself, is this original element, insofar as one is lucid and determined enough to experience it. It is evident that it cannot be an experience possible by means of thought unaware of its own immanence, or still immersed in the dream of its own spiritual being, turned toward spiritual objects. It cannot be tantric thinking but, rather, the most arid, *a-psychic*, abstract thinking and nonetheless capable of being conscious of itself—namely, rationalistic thinking.

There is an intuition of Western idealism, long lost, which, if it had been taken to its logical consequences, could have been able to operate as the Science of the Spirit, namely thinking intuited in its dynamic moment, at that point of consciousness where there emerges, without presuppositions, the sole motive for itself, where it has no need of logic or a gnoseology, in order to be. It is clear that when spiritual seekers attempt to translate this intuition of idealism *into action,* beyond the level of mere speculation, they must abandon the world of reasoning. For them the discipline of meditation, by pure logical transition, is given as necessary. One looks at the sense of *pure thought.* It cannot become experience except as the possession of the dynamic moment of thinking; yet this is ultimately the art of concentration.

The assumption is concentration as a perception of living thinking, not the intellectual or sentimental rumination of a theme placed as an object, which will always inevitably tie the mental movement to the object. If being is not an ideal world in itself, but the idea that rises from a sum of perceptions, how can the meditative act be realized other than as an identity of being and non-being, that is, as a synthesis from a momentary duality, thanks to a springing inner virtue, which nothing presupposes before itself? It is called pure thinking, in that it creates itself by drawing itself from its own universality that continuously becomes identity. It cannot exist prior to creating itself. In the moment it is dialectically determined as a being, as a category, as a concept, it already no longer is; it dies as an abstraction, or as knowledge.

The metaphysical sense of such an identity is that of being valid as the *principle of the synthesis,* that is, as the initial penetration of the most profound category of duality, which *opposes* being to non-being—the category of *eros.* Therefore, it cannot be said that Tantrism offers the pure metaphysical element necessary as the principle of the synthesis. The experience of *eros* is the profound measure of the presence of this (principle), of its unutterable virtue, since it demands as a decisive moment that state of perfect evidence for which thinking is resurrected as being, being in itself, being things—the absolute identity in which the "I" and the world are one. Tantrism presupposes such a synthesis, but with respect to our situation as modern human beings, it does not possess the principle—*it lacks the prime element, the essential immanence.*

The Eastern system that essentially seems to develop the themes of an erotic magic—which responds to the need of the present-day human type—effectively lacks the radical element indispensable to the situation of the fallen human being, namely the movement of cold abstract thought that, having emerged as scientific thinking, conceals within itself the power of a transcendent dimension, recognizable in its pure impersonal nature. Such a metaphysical value, present within the Western scientific experience, escapes both the scientist and the philosopher. In the aridity of agnostic mathematical thinking, a cold light effectively shines, an unnoticed sign of the invisible light of life, closer to the sharp lines of geometry and of formal logic than to the tensions of the yogic or mystical psyche. Such thinking, brought to consciousness and grasped in its non-corporeality, is detected arising from a current of life, whose *dynamis* is precisely what tantric yoga calls *kundalini*.

For Westerners capable of the courage to be modern—that is, to take on their real condition with a conscious act—all that which is represented by reflected thinking cannot but be contingent and illusory, as a product of alienation of thinking's original element. It is a symbolic indication, a numerical or logical assumption of semblance, effectively devoid of a conditioning reality. It is the possibility to form a mental picture, outside any concept of value, or inner engagement, outside moral valuations or the demands of faith, even while able to consider, dispassionately, the themes of morality or of faith. It is abstract mental picturing that does not oblige. In its aridity, it leaves us free. It can attend to everything without binding itself to anything. All that can be thought by means of such thinking is, in fact, *mâyâ*. Therefore, even the dynamic world of Tantrism, with its bold techniques that presume to recapture the original cosmic power, is *mâyâ*.

We, as western investigators, who find ourselves before a picture of the enchanting tantric endeavor, know dispassionately that the thinking by means of which we think it, is a reflection; it is a nothing. If we take action, we know that we deceive ourselves, because our 'mental picturing—*mâyâ*' moves nothing, and any shaktic operation is a movement of the psyche within the psyche and of the psyche imprisoned within the body and of the body not possessed, but which gives a sign of itself through the senses. If we have the courage of such inner positivism, then we are saved. We can attempt *real inner action.*

If reflected thinking is mâyâ, it is nothing; it does not bind to being, nor to existing. At the same time, it is the only activity in which we can freely partake. By means of the lowest but most autonomous vehicle, we *can move outside our own nature,* until contemplating something beyond the corporeal and psychic dynamisms. We can strive toward what we are, beyond sensory existence. We can will this reflected thinking; we can think it. Along the lines of a willful determination, *the thinking that thinks reflected thinking is not reflected,* because it does not need to be reflected to manifest itself objectively. Nevertheless, it actualizes—thanks to the dimension of the reflection—its original impersonality, its *'a-psychicity.'* It is the power within abstract thought that the western physicist-mathematician should have realized, had they been aware of what took place (at the scene of their consciousness) as an inner counterpart of their investigation—far more important than the investigation itself. They will never discover it today, because they lack the intuitive means to understand it. Moreover, within widespread human thinking, something has become sclerotic. That 'dis-individual' element has crossed over into dialectical automatism, into the mediumistic impersonality of the scientist-technician.

For this reason, the task of reintegration, urgently needed by us today, is an ideal that rare human beings recognize. For very few (people), the already-mentioned 'dis-individual' element is still the possibility of the thinking-light that, coldly and intensely willed, awakens the original light of consciousness—its *metaphysical light.* It is the ultimate key, the elementary possibility, the simple absolute of thinking, that it still has available. *If this becomes lost, chaos is inevitable.*

We can briefly say that mathematical-abstract thinking, experienced as such in its initial reflected moment, namely in its moment of impersonality, expresses a power of the soul—the initial flowing of the pure force of the "I." As a reflection free of an objective content, this thinking moves, in its initial moment, within a sphere of impersonal forces, like a pure trace, or a void, in which the metaphysical force of the "I" is potentially present.

No modern scientist or technologist suspects such a possibility inherent within the thinking by means of which they think; for them thinking is real only insofar as it is reflected. The discipline of concentration, which is essentially the experimental method of science applied to the process of knowing, gives way to perceiving thought as an objective entity, whose initial abstract form is *semblance,* namely the only semblance that can be penetrated without transcendences. What—by so thinking—moves within it turns out to be a pure incorporeal entity, not bound, nor binding, existing in itself and, therein, possessing a force that goes beyond the human. One day it will be possible to show how the rising of scientific thought does not have so much the aim of producing a civilization of machines, as of creating the organ of spiritual activity for a new type of human being.

The experience of such an adamantine current of thinking, if translated into knowledge, leads to a perception of the reality of *eros,* which is removed from any vision of it that results from traditional or modern texts, moving from the synthesis that it realizes daily in the immanence of direct knowing. Such a synthesis, perceived and possessed, in its unpredictability, reveals its profound unity with an intact and dynamic primordial element.

The slightest bit that such a path can be intuited allows us to glimpse the urgent need for new spiritual action, not easily conceivable at the current level of consciousness, with respect to which it appears radically transformative. Since this is a subject hard to dialecticize—even if it can be envisaged in logical terms—we will try to approach it by means of the cosmological images of Christian esotericism: images that regard the mystery of the origins. Such a cosmology has its key and an interpretation concerning the new times in the legend of the Grail, whose hidden meaning cannot be provided by any critical investigation, even of an esoteric order, but only by a direct imaginative contemplation of symbolic representations—a contemplation for whose technique and specific references to the treated theme, we refer to our book, *Dell'Amore Immortale.*

The magic of *eros* demands to be removed from the conception of a propitiatory function of a higher advent of the ego or of the empowerment of human beings who have become one with their own limitations. *Solar magic* exists, but it has quite another function than that of conferring powers to those of us desirous of life. From the pages that follow, it can so happen, among other things, that there is no higher faculty in us, like intuition, charity, courage, loyalty, fidelity, that can express itself in its fullness, without freeing itself from a radical bond, which is *eros*—not sex, but the longing inherent in it.

The religiosity that could once provide ritualistically the compensating inner counterpart of such a radical subjection, provided that it does not possess the corresponding knowledge, has exhausted its task. As things currently stand, no traditional or mystical compensation turns out to be valid, but this does not mean that the remedy lies in deriving benefits from fundamental bondage, and to that end providing it with higher meanings, as it occurs today in certain aberrations of a mediumistic-orgiastic type or of a psychedelic soggy dullness. Instead, the task is to actualize the forces of consciousness of the fallen level, so as to glimpse what determines it, to the point of identifying the radical servitude. This conceals the highest secret, which is revealed to a consciousness capable of being consistent with its own principle, in itself not subjectable to bondage of any kind, whatever the level of the fall may be. In that sense, the task turns out to be viable as an enterprise of overcoming the human, whose scheme can be contemplated in the symbolism of the Grail, if we are able to recognize the need for action that goes beyond what can be deduced from the imaginative structure of the myth concerning the mystery of our future, the weft of metaphysical forces that operate in such a structure.

2.

ANDROGYNY AND EDEN

In Gnostic texts, the figure of Isis presents two symbolic valences of the same content, mutually opposed—one that is lower, dark, related to physical generation, the other that is higher, celestial, signifying metaphysical generation—namely, Isis-Hecate and Isis-Sophia. We will see how Isis-Sophia sums up both of them, she being both the true Isis, and Hecate her veil. The metaphysical generation contains, within itself, the physical one.

The figure of Isis-Sophia can be recognized in the image of the Virgin, which has the Moon and the Serpent at her feet. Isis-Hecate, apart from the myth, can be derived from the Moon's dynamic function in relation to sex, to fertilization, and to menstruation. The cosmological connection can be grasped from traditions regarding the history of the development of the twofold human nature—masculine and feminine—and of the corresponding sexual necessity, in response to an event that can be identified as Moon's separation from the Earth. The development of the two natures—masculine and feminine—from the crisis of the original androgenic entity, sexual necessity, fertilization, and birth are processes that can be contemplated consequent to that of the lunar body's separation from the Earth. The epoch of such separation is preceded by that of the Sun's separation from the Earth.

There is a moment in primordial human history that corresponds to the period when the Earth, the Sun and the Moon still formed a single celestial body. The solar part represents the spiritual element most independent of the physical manifestation; the lunar part (represents) the densest element that renders such a manifestation possible. The Earth is in a sort of dynamic equilibrium between these two polarities. Corresponding to the solar-lunar duality on Earth is the human structure that equally bears the two principles Sun-Moon according to a power of synthesis, the embryo of the androgenic structure, which would even manifest corporeally, after the Sun's detachment from the Earth. Prior to such a detachment, the human being consisted of two parts, a higher (part) in which flow solar forces, and a lower (part), demanding the action of even stronger forces, which elaborate the densest matter to draw the corporeal form from it.

As a result of the Sun's detachment from the Earth, human beings gathered within themselves the innermost molding powers to reproduce on their own such a corporeal form, which was originally the structure of Androgyny. The possibility for human beings to draw the androgynous being out of themselves arose from the Sun's influence that operates from outside the Earth and from the influence of the Moon still united with the Earth.

The Mystery of Androgyny can be contemplated as a moment of our formative power as human beings, which arose from our ability to gather forces more elevated and, therefore, more profound, relative to the lunar element strengthened on the physical plane by the Sun's separation from the Earth. The currents capable of ruling the lower lunar element would be recognizable in the aforementioned symbol of the Virgin that corresponds to the aspect of the Isis-Sophia. We will see during the course of the present study how the path toward restoring Androgyny's radical force is the undertaking alluded to in the saga of the Grail and likewise corresponds to the symbol of Isis-Sophia. This (Isis-Sophia), in fact, takes on and redeems within itself the tenebrous Hecate. We will see, in any case, why woman holds the keys to the reintegration of man (so that the Virgin would be called *Janua Coeli)* and how the present civilization can risk permanently losing the sense of such a reintegration, by reducing woman to man's erotic companion, or to a mere begetter of children.

The separation of the sexes, as the loss of the androgynous unity, results from the terrestrial-lunar element's prevalence within the human being, which the original transcendent forces oppose, giving an order to the initial experience of the couple.

As long as the process of human consciousness coincided with the order of such forces, the need of the powerful lower lunar powers would be controlled by human beings and used as a physical generating virtue.

The original harmony restored at a lower level by the human couple, following the diversification of the sexes, itself underwent a crisis due to the gradual prevalence of the lower lunar element, after the Moon's separation from the Earth, the relationship now being entrusted to the human being's capacity to harmonize the solar (masculine) element with the lunar (feminine) element. It is the moment in which the human being succumbs to the seduction of Lucifer.

The Moon's separation from the Earth means that the governing forces of the lower lunar element now act directly on the Moon (that) separated from the Earth. In this respect, one can intuit the mystery of the human beings' reintegration. The possibility for us (as human beings) to resolve within ourselves the innermost infernal element lies in our connection to the relationship of forces whose key and symbol is the Moon.

After the separation, the occult relationship with the Moon would continue on the human plane by means of the woman; *woman would, from then on, hold the keys to the work of human resurrection.* Thanks to the survival of the celestial androgynous element in her, alongside the need for reproductive functions, woman would continue to maintain the human species' relationship with the extrasensory powers of the Moon, thereby simultaneously assuming, within her inner-corporeal constitution, the dual function of Isis—celestial and infernal. In the saga of the Grail, the re-consecration of the Castle and the celestial Tabernacle appeals to the intervention of the same female figure responsible for the fall of Amfortas. Thus, Gerbert of Mostreuil explains Parsifal's initial moment of helplessness by his having forgotten his own woman.

When the Sun separated from the Earth, the formative forces of light, which until then had operated from within the higher structure of human beings, became inadequate for their relationship with the inferior part of this (structure), traversed by the Earth's lunar currents—namely, currents that, in order to distance themselves from the element that governs them, could exercise a deeper solidifying action of the human form. The lunar currents are necessary for human beings to root themselves within the lower region of the earth. Such currents would become the dynamic substance of their self-reproductive process, in that each human being would meet these lunar currents with a power of synthesis native to them: hence the androgynous form.

Through the Sun's separation from the Earth, the lunar currents acquired a decisive power over human beings. Thus, higher spiritual forces intervened to safeguard the equilibrium of the relationship between the higher human being and the lower human being—forces whose power is such that they can descend as organizers into the lunar depths. Those depths constitute the infernal region of the Earth, or the region of the *inferior waters,* where the highest forces operate through the power of the sound ether. They permeate the lower liquid earth and, therefore, that of its dynamis present in the human structure, according to the power of a transcendent harmony that would express itself as a generative virtue of the androgynous human being and, later, when even the Moon would become separated from the Earth, as a generating virtue of the original human couple, still without sin. Such transcendent harmony is the original element of human love, which the couple would gradually forget with time. One day the first Greek philosophers would recognize the echo of this transcendent harmony of the universe's rhythmic imprint and would evoke it as the *music of the spheres.*

The "music of the spheres," which, in the visible firmament manifests as the rhythm of the stars, flowed in the original androgynous human being and in the subsequent human couple as a magical power that we do not possess within ourselves since we gather it as a transcendent gift. We would lose this gift over time; it would remain within us, by means of the generative functions, but it would be extraneous to waking consciousness and to our inner perception. From then on, the purpose of our lives would be to recapture this lost good through our own power and, therefore, to know its content by means of the emerging forces of consciousness. We will discover this lost good as our creative force when we become capable of glimpsing the non-terrestrial stream of self-consciousness now bound to the earthly; that is, when we become capable of perceiving, beyond the semblance of the mechanical universe, the music that minimally resounds within earthly love, tragically contradicted—namely, the echo of the harmony of the spheres.

This primordial history of the human being, which unsurprisingly is the history of a cosmic-human love relationship, demanded to be freed from the prejudice of restorations of the original accord that later was possible to realize, by means of the Initiations and the Mysteries of the various traditions, because in any case *human affairs have since then unfolded according to a continuous loss of level, with respect to the primordial condition.* Since then, the only value worth speaking about is the rise of an "I" aware of itself, not through the exhausted traditional impulses but, rather, through thought and experience demanding the supra-sensory as an individual activity directed toward the sensory. Based on the awareness of such an individual element and on its inner virtue of self-redemption, we can in time recognize as legitimate the vocation of a resurrection of the original human element. This element has been naturally compromised by all the confusions of resurrecting the Tradition's dead forms—a Tradition that, as we have shown elsewhere, is no longer even the shadow of what the Sacred Science of primeval times, or perennial Spiritual Science, was and is.

The mystery of the human couple's original accord is the reference point that we need to assume as a measure of the inanity and of the fallacy of all the forms of recovery of the spiritual by means of initiations and sexual ceremonies to which one inevitably turns with complete estrangement from the celestial element of the original binomial, which possesses the "great mystery" of the Androgyny. Actually, in such ceremonies, the soul of the initiand* moves, led forth by a partial supra-sensory vision, or a vision limited by the original luciferic imprint and which, therefore, tends toward blessedness or toward a liberation, themselves conditioned by the hidden demand of desire. Such desire can be seen either by the still uncontaminated "I," or by the "I" capable of exhausting the contamination. But it is important that this "I" be there, because *it alone bears something more than what can be learned from books, or from*

---

*   a person about to be initiated

traditions, namely an element of life that was at the beginning, and that, even if it never ceased to be, has been able to operate directly in human beings only when it could manifest as the *I am*, in an earthly body, and in a human personality, according to an Event that, to be the resolving event, is *the most hidden* that exists—unconsciously de-realized precisely by those who have presumed to represent it in the world.

Earthly love is an obscure attempt to reconnect the "I am" with its source. Therefore, an initiatic *eros* is the undertaking that can spring from the "I" that realizes, within itself, the "I am." It cannot be the attainment of sexual rites or of magical ceremonies or practices, where any possible liberation of the force is not attributable to its *principle* but, rather, only to the profound longing opposed to it.

The spirit—as will be shown—cannot be sought in sex. On the contrary, sex must be sought in the spirit. The image of the mystery of the original couple presupposes an understanding of the meaning required for a magic of love. In the type of love that unites the original couple, flowing from a unity complete in itself—a synthesis of superhuman powers—in the sublimity of such a love, one can have a sure reference to the understanding of the initiatic experience of *eros.* Above all, one can understand how such an experience is indistinguishable from Initiation itself, as a possibility restored by the "I am."

The human being's original story is presented as a mystery of the relationship that the primordial couple possesses and then loses, through the process of physicalization, whose initial phase allows for its formation. This formation itself nonetheless leads to the loss of a prior higher unity. It is not hard to notice how the sense of such a relationship still remains the enigma of our present-day history. Human life gravitates around the power of *eros,* like around a force that encroaches on the transcendence and sinks into sensory categories, so that whoever is capable of receiving it only in such an inferior expression, fixes its inverse universality (Freud) as a value, by impeding not only the contemplation of its transcendence, but by cooperating in the permanence of human beings in *the state of cognitive impotence regarding their greatest problem.*

The lower aspect of sex is a psychic human production.

It is not about sex. Initially, the issue of sex is not a reality of the soul but, rather, a direct activity of the Spirit within human corporeality. It can be said that, at first, the soul is limited to a calm reception of the relationship that the Spirit has with the reproductive sphere. When the Sun separated from the Earth, the power of the forces of sound, or of the *Word,* and of life, over the *lower darkness*, made us capable of generating our own likeness by ourselves. Within our structure, the forces of light (the principle of consciousness), the *higher waters* (astral body) and the *lower waters* (lunar body), or lower astral—the presence within us of the world that would later constitute the Moon—are held together by the principle of sound and of life, as if by a higher "I." The creative synthesis of the forces of light-life and of darkness, governed by the power of the Word, is present in us as an androgynous power, which made our nature binomial, capable of generating our own likeness. The part of our structure by means of which androgynous human beings are able to reproduce themselves—in that they gather the Powers of the creative sound within it—is the lower part of the body, the seat of the lunar currents.

The lower zone of the "inferior waters," or the lunar zone, was that part of the earthly sphere that acquired overwhelming power from the moment of the Sun's detachment to that in which the highest Powers also detached the Moon from the Earth. This is the moment when darkness was enlivened by its own radical *vis* (power) and could work towards a densification of the human form, where the forces of the light-life ceased to have the original control of its lower part. It was the time of the *destitution of the Androgynous*, or of the separation of the sexes. To maintain our androgynous equilibrium as human beings, the Powers of sound that ruled the lower part would have to replace our consciousness by operating within the higher part. But this would arrest our development as human beings, whose task would be to develop individual forces in order to acquire the powers of our higher nature, thus far given to us. Therefore, while the separation of the sexes was taking place, those powers would continue operating within us, independently of our consciousness. The *life* within us still cooperated with the *light*, to the degree in which one's relation with the other half of the couple distanced itself from sex. Gradually, we, however, tended to connect ourselves by way of the sensory with the lower sphere of the body, in which the harmony of the light and of the life (by virtue of the forces of the Word) made the reproductive act possible. The connection with sex by way of the sensory path *caused the forces of light to lose the cooperation of the forces of life.*

It was the opportunity of the Serpent, the symbol of the degenerate human form, due to the advantage of the lower watery earth over the forces of light, namely the beginning of the activity of thinking as *light without life*, which would later become the *light's dead reflection*—dialectics. The original Powers of life and of sound, at this point, directly ruled the dark part of the Earth, which they had detached from this (Earth), to create the lunar body—the lower fragment of the Earth, whose expulsion is alluded to in the myth of the celestial entities' victorious struggle with the Serpent, or with the Dragon. Since then, the Moon would be the symbol of our lowest nature, governed by the solar powers, which by now would not be able to operate similarly within our souls, except *through our free actions.*

We will one day defeat the Serpent, to the extent that we are able to reclaim our spiritual nature. To realize and to conquer the Serpent's nature will be an initiatic symbol. In that sense, to the spiritual eye, the Moon, characterizing the period of the Serpent and the loss of the androgynous power, assumes importance as a symbol of the endeavor, so that our heavenly constitution can be restored if we succeed in carrying out the synthesis of our lower and higher natures—to the extent that we can reawaken (out of this synthesis) the power of redemption within ourselves, which is the redemption of the lunar body that governs our sexual lives and the mechanism of the generative function.

The resurrection of such power—to whose loss the sensual bond of earthly love, the need of egoism, sickness and death are related—is visible in the symbol of the Virgin that stands on the crescent of the moon with the Serpent beneath her feet. It is as if the Virgin freed herself in the heavens by virtue of the Moon purged of the Serpent's shame, so that the luminous crescent is the celestial Monstrance, or the Chalice of the Last Supper, that gives itself as a symbol of the human being's radical liberating force.

This radical force truly bears the serpentine movement within itself. These are dominating powers of the lower liquid earth—namely, of the Earth's lunar element, those that gave us the possibility of androgynous generation (or self-generation) before the lunar prevarication and the consequent detachment of the tenebrous Earth or of the sub-terrestrial part from the Earth itself. These are the very forces that separated the lunar body from the Earth, not because they did not dominate the lunar darkness, but because human beings began not to dominate them. Therefore, the Serpent does not arise by way of such forces, but by way of the human being. The Archangel Michael pursues the Dragon through the human being.

In essence, the loss of Eden was not a state that concerned the Earth or the Moon, or the Serpent, but only the human being, and not the human as a spiritual being but, rather, the soul of the human being, where all the forces, higher and lower, that operated at the beginning are present. The sense of such history is *the mystery of the human soul,* namely the possibility for the spirit to fructify it. Human beings still lack its range, the form that corresponds to the Spirit, because they still have not realized the spiritual principle within the soul. The soul's separation from the spirit and the reflected spiritual form in which the soul believes it has an "I" or a spirit within itself, perpetuate—on the individual plane—the loss of a level whose memory we have even come to lose, as well as the possibility of conceiving a conscious recovery of it.

3.

THE HEAVENLY WOMAN

The forces of the Word that order the lower element of the Earth (Moon) through the sound ether, operate—as a creative virtue of the androgynous being—on the same element present within the human being. They continue to operate on each component of the human couple when this couple is formed from the fall of the androgynous being into the sphere of sexual necessity. However destitute the level, the emerging human dyad still possesses the pattern of the celestial generation.

In the original couple, those forces still governed, *by means of enchantment,* the power of the Serpent necessary for generation in the physical sphere, or the sphere of the "lower waters," through the union of the couple's bodies—masculine and feminine. In effect, the Serpent is still enchanted by the force of the *music of the spheres.* Yet, it does not have power over the higher part of the human being. It cannot be the enchanter of human consciousness, since this (consciousness) lives off its own gift of light. The light's virtue maintains its extra-human communion with the forces of life and of sound, or of the Word, which govern the sphere of the "lower waters." This would be the secret of the original couple's accord, founded on a first divine event, which has in it all the power of the future, regardless of its development.

The secret of the original accord that only Initiates from then on were able to understand would enclose within itself the perennial pattern of the couple's union, intangible through mutual bewilderment and the millenary search along the equivocation of prostitution. Each tragic expression of the couple's earthly love, like the impotent pursuit of a lost higher good, would henceforth be the unconscious yearning toward the pattern of the

Primordial Arcane, which one day, if human beings discover the dignity of knowledge, would restore their original nature. They would be able to encounter within themselves the serpentine nature, which would no longer need enchantment, having been vanquished within the human sphere by the Redeemer.

Such a victory would itself be a Mystery inaccessible to human consciousness, since it is the correlation of the Logos to the earthly world and to human nature, namely *the correlation impenetrable to rational knowledge*—to knowledge that we attain from being subjected to the Serpent. Therefore, redemption is not a gratuitous or mythical gift, as some current esotericists believe, who apparently reject it for the sake of their fundamental autonomy, while they are reverentially prepared to accept any transmission of power from Indian or Islamic teachers.

The gift of the Redeemer remains inaccessible to both religious and esoteric individuals, whose knowledge, resulting from the Serpent's activity, is incapable of identifying, within itself, the perpetuation of such activity and does not actualize the conversion of itself, which only the gift is able to actualize. *In order to be gathered, the gift of the Redeemer demands the greatest autonomy of awareness, the most radical individualism.* It demands overcoming the limit of dialectics and of fear—the inner act that is essentially sacrificial. For the situation of those who shun such a gift, there is no other explanation than the fear of having to gather, within oneself, a higher force—namely, that of the "I." It is a fear of opening up to the superhuman, the fear of losing the limit of the contingent "I," that is to say, the fear of being the "I."

Since desire results in the loss of the human couple's original accord, and since knowledge arises as a higher fruit from desire 'sinking its roots' into human beings, the reintegration cannot begin except as *an event of knowledge.* In knowing, we have the faculty that has arisen as a consequence of the "original sin," but simultaneously the initial possibility of conversion. The possibility of the light's restoration is inherent in the reflected light of thought. *Metanoia* pertains to human freedom, since it is the volitional accord of the consciousness soul with the spirit. For this reason, the human couple potentially possesses within itself the germ for the restoration of the superhuman couple.

The sin is not sex, since, originally, the separation of the bodies into male and female, and the consequent need for their sexual union, is not a separation of souls. The power of Androgyny is still present in the union of the couple's souls. *When the souls' union falters, the actual fall of the human being begins.* Human self-consciousness would arise from the fact that the soul would no longer recognize itself in the other.

The original couple still bears the angelic archetype that operates by way of the soul; its secret is allowing the union of the sexes to come about through a divine process, which occurs by virtue of the Serpent's enchanting Powers, which can operate undisturbed during the couple's intercourse. This intercourse occurs according to a *sanctity*, safeguarded by the fact that the couple is in a state of profound sleep with respect to it. The couple's waking state as a harmony, or unequivocal music, of the souls is extraneous to the sexual act. This (sexual act) would become sinful, the day that their waking state inevitably arose. It is the path of consciousness toward self-consciousness. It leads mental picturing and willing to an inner separation in each individual's soul, while imposing an ever-tighter relationship of it with the sensory world, which needs above all the individualization of mental picturing. In extra-conscious willing, the two souls would still feel the profound willing, but the activity of mental picturing would begin to divide them. This mental picturing would gradually coincide with sensory appearing, until it could no longer be distinguished from it.

Once the couple ceased to see each other with a spiritual eye and to realize their encounter as a sacred exchange of soul forces, they *became conditioned by the images of their bodies.* The vision of the other as a being unique in its complementarity— which summarized within itself the whole masculine or feminine species—was replaced by the appearance of the physical figure, which, valued as such, lost the sense of uniqueness. On the physical plane, in fact, one corporeal shape is as good as another. By seeking individuality in the bodily appearance of the other, we humans lost ourselves in the species, that is, in animality. *We could not but betray the original accord.*

The beholding of the physical shape of the other (partner), is a soul movement that no longer encounters the soul beyond corporeality. In the Edenic phase, the original movement of the soul toward the soul was the surviving androgynous correlation, whereby the fluidic body was one with the fluidic body of the other, through the complementarity of the masculine-feminine element of the one with the feminine-masculine element of the other. Physicality did not constitute the membrane. Rather, it was the means for the spiritual act of the soul in the correlation of the two (partners). When the beholder encounters only the physical being of the other, the soul's spiritual movement is arrested at a representation that demands the correlation at a level where the other does not exist, but simply *appears*. *Longing* is the soul binding, by way of spiritual forces, to the 'appearing', or to a mental picturing that no longer perceives the spirit. It is a longing that will always be disappointed, because it actually seeks the supra-sensory, (while) believing that it desires the sensory.

The spirit lives in the semblance, but it is negated. It manifests, but it is alienated. When human beings stop perceiving the reality of others beyond semblance, they lose the sense of the other's *unique value*, or of the universal, which, summarizing within that person the whole of masculinity or the whole of femininity, has the power to overcome the semblance. From that moment, each semblance would appear to us as the universal that we seek, but there would be no coincidence between the semblance and its corresponding universal, because we would no longer have the inner organ capable of perceiving it. We would seek it through another being, also apparent as a corporeal being and, as such, an impenetrable semblance of the universal of which that person is a vestment. As a symbol of disappointed longing, the body would nonetheless always be the arouser of desire, the vehicle of the magic of *eros*: which would undoubtedly play by means of spiritual forces but without, however, possessing their principle, since this magic was inexorably outside their original circuit.

Once the other person's bodily appearance was equated with their being—namely, with the universal that urges unknown within the soul and whose power and nostalgia it feels—the one would encounter the other, nonetheless, *always thanks to soul forces*, striving at times toward the original communion, which, with rare exceptions, could not be realized because of the separation of androgynous forces at the level of consciousness where longing is generated. Thus, in the bodies' encounter the couple would seek something that such an encounter was unable to provide. The encounter would be erotic, intellectual, sentimental. It would thus use forces of the soul that would remain unknown, which each person would believe to have found in the other, having identified it with the corporeal being— its outer symbol.

The tragic aspect of all human love would, from then on, consist of each person, through the forces of their souls, tending towards the corporeality of the other, believing they seek the soul, eternal love, devotion, and fidelity. Prostitution, as a psychic inclination that tends to appear as normal, would be the consequence of the pursuit of the good lost by means of the bodies' varied experience, up to that sad desiccation of the sacred meaning of the feminine figure that would reduce it to a mere instrument of pleasure, making of this very desecration the means for a ceremonialism formally sacred, or for rites of erotic magic. The misunderstanding of such rites would be the belief of being able to possess the aroused forces, by means of the fluid orientations of longing and the specific forms of the sexual act—forces that cannot be subjugated to a principle engaged, from the outset, by the longing of which it presumes to take advantage. One cannot open the passage to an absolute, trans-humanizing act, if, to this end, one utilizes the forces to which one has become subservient and whose profound impulse is to impede the passage.

Understanding how the loss of the human couple's original harmony is connected to the fall of humanity (all the way to the extreme consequences of a vision of life that excludes the spirit) has become more arduous than ever. The real danger is that today's inner human being becomes unable to conceive the value of such an original accord.

The reintegration of human dignity, the salvation of culture and civilization, the restoration of the hierarchy of values and of real fraternity, are ideals that cannot have meaning or the power of life, where the accord—whose secret is held by the human couple—cannot be conceived. In fact, the *forgotten archetype* tends to live again in the relationship of the couple. Man can find the spiritual woman; woman can find the spiritual man. This is the possibility of the new times, to the extent that forgetfulness can be assumed as a condition of the awareness open to each and every possibility beyond itself. Right at the point where we have arrived, the path of reintegration can be the greatest need, like a final determination. Such a path—if it arouses in investigators the decision to overcome the limit, which is the limit of individual consciousness—gradually reveals to them its coincidence with the task of *rediscovering the lost etheric accord.* The theme of the inner woman, or of celestial love, appears to them as a foundational condition alongside the possibility to effectively encounter the being of sacred love, the only one, *the original bride rediscovered,* and yet, to them the bearer of the ineffable content of the Grail.

It is said that the key of the accord is our hidden connection to a system of cosmic equilibriums, of which the Moon is the support and symbol. Woman on Earth continues to maintain an ancient relationship with the Moon. She possesses the connection, to the extent that the transcendent principle, which in the Moon permeates and rules lower matter, is present in her as the soul's constitutive element, operating right down to the physical structure. Such a structure, beheld in its simple sensory appearance, is illusory. but it is also the symbol of what the human soul has lost or forgotten. Therefore, man, in looking at a woman, has the feeling of having before him the being that can restore the lost higher world. Through the figure of her, he feels surfacing the hope of the resurrection of a degree of bliss and purity, of which present-day existence is a deprivation.

Beyond her sensory appearance, one can have a presentiment within woman of a supra-natural power that can kill or re-enliven, depending on the relationship that man's inner principle is able to establish with it. This hidden value of woman is decisive for the undertaking of reintegration, where it is drawn to the concept of the instrumentality of the feminine being for magic operations of an aphroditic type, proper to certain Eastern and Western schools, which presume to possess the knowledge of such hidden value. In reality, they do not possess it.

The mystery hidden in the figure of the woman as the bearer of reintegration, or as the destroyer, can be intuited in the light of the metaphysical notion of Androgyny; a secret truth revealed as a decisive illumination, in this respect, is the feminine character of the Androgynous figure, or of the originally masculine-feminine being, bearer of the animic (soul) synthesis of the solar-lunar forces. *The metaphysical configuration of the Androgyny is feminine.* In the woman, the highest possibility of a reintegrating magic survives, in virtue of its specific soul-bodily structure. This does not mean that the original androgynous being conformed to the features of femininity—which would be a substantial contradiction—but that woman, because of her animic (soul) being's relationship with the corporeal sheath, unconsciously actualizes the nature of androgyny. For in her, the soul's androgynous entity has an autonomy with respect to corporeality that man does not possess. Man's soul is more inserted in the physical structure than that of the woman. This relational difference is transmitted to the etheric body, which, being masculine in the woman, has the androgynous consonance with the corresponding part of the soul, as is not possible for man's etheric body, (which is) more adherent and thus subservient to physical corporeality.

This unconscious androgynous element that emerges in the physical form, thanks to the etheric body's relative independence from physicality, makes woman an angel-like or deific symbol in man's eyes, awakening resonances of remote blessings. But man ignores the content of the symbol; he does not recognize having before him a living symbol, or even a sensually impenetrable reality. The androgynous element demands to be re-awakened and returned to its magical function at a time when the function of forgetfulness, or of the fall, appears exhausted.

The theme of "celestial love" returns at a time in which the traditional, or mystical, or providential direction of earthly love is definitively lost; at a time when human individuality, arising in the form demanded by the experience of the lowest degree of being—the sensory—runs the risk of losing the "human state"; at a time when human beings can put in doubt every higher meaning of life and thus of human love, the couple's sacredness of marriage, the esoteric sense of monogamy, while the priests themselves assert a right to the gratification of the senses, believing it to be a corporeal right and revealing that they dismiss (the fact) that longing does not exist in the body, but only in the soul.

At a time when we cease to be guided by the Spirit, the supra-sensory impulse of the times asks us for the initiative to discover the Spirit within us. At the lowest level of descent into the earthly realm, (the fact) that we no longer receive spiritual directions transcendent to us demands from us the *animadversio* (observation) of the danger of losing our humanity, but it simultaneously means that the time has come for us to demand that we make contact with the fundamental forces of our individuality. These forces are the very ones that once ruled our lunar body. They are the same ones that, having separated the Sun from the Earth, allowed the power of the Serpent to position itself at the threshold of the sexual sphere, as the guardian of the mystery of procreation.

These forces of life and of sound rule the Serpent, but they cannot remove from it what we have allowed with our soul's adherence to the sensory categories. The moment of becoming aware of this original history, present in its timelessness, in the current human structure, must be regarded as having been reached, if the echo of the spiritual that helped the fallen human being now appears spent: and there seems to be no spiritualism or esotericism of the fallen human being, which today can offer us a path to grasp the real meaning of our history.

4.

THE LUNAR STONE

The epoch of the "I" is that which manifests below what we, through profound determination, can rediscover above. Human individuality, in itself, has a force of ascension that comes to it from becoming self-conscious in the lowest form— the sensory one.

Through the force lying deep within it to the point of transcendence, the "I" has the capacity to discover the loftiness that belongs to it as an original condition. But such a possibility escapes the "I," because its origin is hidden from it by the sensory form of the articulation of its force within earthliness. Modern-day humans cannot conceive of realizing the force apart from the sensory form, while the reality of the force is precisely what it is beyond the limit of the form in which it appears, as in a symbol.

The force's limit expresses itself in mental picturing, which is identified with the sensory form, unaware of being able to move before or beyond it. Longing is the impulse to identify mental picturing with sensory appearing. *The separation of the original androgynous element can be seen as a separation of thinking from willing.* Thinking, separated from its own internal force, tends to find this force outside itself. Its deprivation becomes a longing for the object, which would be outside it, and as such valid—namely, sensory appearing. By identifying with its own object, mental picturing subjects the life of the soul to the sensory realm—with which the subtle relationship is the longing. Longing is the substratum of consciousness. Consciousness will be able to free itself from this subjection only when it manages to see (within the sensory realm) not a fundamental world— valid in itself and that even moves history—but, rather, the consequence of its own deprivation; and yet, it will appeal to its own principle, so that it can take on the longing impulse and restore it as the articulation of its force.

The channel of the spirit within us is traversed by longing. The spirit's current in such a channel becomes longing. Once the original couple starts to become aware of the functions of bodily nature—to which it was previously foreign—longing, together with knowledge, emerges by means of it. The human couple is expelled from Paradise, which is to say, it is expelled from its own vital or etheric body; it falls into the physical body. *The life of willing is separated from the light of thinking.* This light becomes reflected. Lacking life, it realizes its own being as reflection. The soul's bond to the reflection is longing. Nevertheless, from here on, the power of the "I" as spirit contains the secret of its own resurrection, given that its force continuously shows up hidden within longing, which is the life that escaped from the light and obtusely reunited with the reflection. The reflection becomes the isolator of longing if it is lived as pure reflection, or pure thinking, by the "I." It then unites with a life, which is not desire, but its original light of life. One has in such a case the experience of the soul's resurgence from a state of death—the beginning of a true resurrection.

Longing is the spirit's substance, by means of which the soul falls into apparent death, which is the oblivion of its Edenic structure, namely the oblivion of the light's accord with life. Nevertheless, in that very alienation, that is, in the possibility that reflected light allows itself to be contemplated as a death, the principle of the appearance's resolution, or of the disenchantment of death, is present. The soul's apparent death, as a condition of longing, is the source of the world's *mâyâ. Mâyâ conceals the magic of the resurrection.*

From this apparent death, which is the privation of the spirit, the soul projects its own dis-animation onto the world, which arises before it as an objective and opposite alterity. From this death, the resurrection has its secret in the same current of longing, whose channel below is *eros,* and above is reflected (or dialectical) thought—the expression of dis-animation. *Dialectics* is the codification of longing. Therefore, the Serpent has two heads—one above and one below—in mental picturing and in willing. This amounts to saying that we have two adversaries. But with respect to the possibility of overturning the current of desire, by means of the soul's resurrection, they constitute a synthetic adversarial force, which assumes different aspects according to the place within the soul where we attempt to liberate ourselves. Likewise, by reality's mutual correspondence to the symbol, those of us who presently aspire to reconnect with the Mysteries of the West—which today resume the past function of the East—must be able to recognize two fearsome adversaries of the Grail, two admirably articulated doctrines, which have the task of deviating our research (by indicating a false path toward the heart of the Mysteries) and of paralyzing our forces forever.

The Art of the Ancient Adversary is to operate within the human being, within the vehicle of those soul forces by means of which we identify with corporeality and with the sensory (realm) in order to have self-awareness, so as to believe ourselves to be free. Such soul forces, impersonal and powerful in themselves, are alienated within the current of longing, namely the longing within thinking, the longing within feeling, the longing within willing—from the *dialectics* that builds culture to the *sex* that nourishes the infernal level. (Indeed, sex degrades culture, not so much by providing it with content, but by operating within us as a power that paralyzes the pure intuitive forces necessary to the process of culture).

The art of the Ancient Adversary is to keep the thinking forces separate from those of willing within the current of desire, so that we remain unaware of their synthesis, which is the principle of the inner androgynous restoration—*mental picturing* (or imagining) being the feminine polarity, and *willing* the masculine one. The inner reconstitution of the original synthesis—which one day will be able to be realized as the restoration of our adamantine structure—is the principle of sacred love.

Therefore, the art of the ancient Serpent is to operate in the areas of the soul where, through the current of desire, it can give rise in us to the illusion that we can choose for ourselves, causing us to exchange for our lives the state of deep sleep, proper to the lunar body, or the apparent death by means of which, minerally, we take on the world, the series of appearances, including the appearance of the other. Desire produces the appearance. It needs the appearance in order to subsist. The play of appearances is, in fact, the chance for the Serpent to propose life's ideals or motives to us—from love to compassion, to freedom, to spiritualism, to power, to religiosity.

Where the Ancient Adversary keeps the two forces of mental picturing and of willing separate within the soul, it can control us. It impedes us from actualizing the "I" that possesses, within itself, intact, the original androgynous power. It manages to make us live within the "'I's" reflection, there, where the "I" lives fragmented in a thousand forms of reflection, one opposing the other, while we believe ourselves to be in each form where the reflection flashes to us our ideal of life, or our creed, or our mysticism, or our esotericism. Within the current of unobserved desire, it manages to make us turn to a sexual magic, to an erotic ritualism, gifted also with chrisms of the Tradition and of present-day *dialectics*.

Actually, none of us can counter desire, even when we oppose it, because no one effectively glimpses where it arises. And if it is innate to the "I," it cannot be its non-manifestation that overcomes such desire, because all activities of the "I" nevertheless manifest it. The truth is that it has nothing really to do with the "I" but, rather, with its reflection, with its contingent presence. It is this contingent presence that the Obstructer strengthens by using the power of the "I." Our predicament is to find the "I" to which we refer; to notice that each of us speaks about the "I," as if we really were it.

The path to rediscovering the "I" is sacred love, since it is the force that draws consciousness into the unknown area of the soul, toward an absolute point. It is the path of loyalty and of dedication to the *inner being, which reveals itself in the other (partner)*. The movement of sacred love flows forth from the "I," as the supra-conscious impulse of consciousness for pursuing the eternal, that is, for seeking the very "I," whose enigma is alluded to in the symbolism of the Grail stone. Each of us who moves according to sacred love, seeks our higher "I" in the other half of the couple, because only within it can the "I" be found. The "I" bears within itself, restored, the virtue of overcoming the human, the androgynous secret of the soul. The task is to notice the point where the activity of the "I" expresses its secret within the soul, a transcendence that is the path by means of which the soul finally awakens from its apparent death.

Present within the human soul are all those forces that operated in the beginning, including the forces of the Serpent, from which the dominion of the primordial life current is safeguarded, until the "I" awakens within itself the forces that have fundamentally defeated the Serpent. It is ultimately the task of the "I" to actualize the gift of the Redeemer. Parsifal discovers this when on Holy Friday he understands the sense of his long pilgrimage and of his invincibility in combat.

The task is to discover that the Serpent is defeated within us, within the original vital (etheric) body that has remained intact, outside the current of desire in which reflected consciousness moves. The undertaking of the Grail consists in rediscovering the life of the light intact within the human being—an undertaking equal to that of overcoming reflected consciousness. In reality, it has to do with overcoming what normally is considered human. Sacred love realizes such an undertaking, because it is the soul's movement that overcomes the sphere of consumption and of death, through the love of the Spirit, which is the being of the other partner.

The undertaking of sacred love occurs in the couple's interiority, according to an inner surge of a will aimed at overcoming the individual limit. Such *willing* essentially rediscovers its unity with *thinking*. Therefore, it overcomes the limit of reflected consciousness, until encountering the *luminous sound* of the Edenic vital (etheric) body, that guards the secret of the original correlation, or of supra-human love, which alone can redeem us. It bears the power of the ancient creative music, of which the soul is essentially structured, from which the soul estranged itself in order to extricate itself in reflected consciousness. The correlation of the supra-human couple is rediscovered as a dimension of consciousness resounding according to the etheric archetype, whose restitution is symbolized by the *solar diamond* drawn from the *lunar stone*—the precious content of the Grail, of whose hidden meaning no rational thought, or erudite esotericism, can become aware.

The birth of the "I," in the age of the consciousness soul,

occurs as the emergence of a principle that is able to unify the two forces—thinking and willing. If we can recognize the sign of the loss of the original androgynous power in the splitting of such forces, we can likewise comprehend how their synthesis is a condition of human reintegration. The power of synthesis is the virtue of the original vital (etheric) body.

The current of life split from the current of knowledge is the will that expires into the longing by means of which we will illusorily, since we never achieve our objective. The activity of mental picturing, split from the current of willing, is the dialectical thinking that provides desire with the nourishment of the world's semblances: not of the world's reality, but of its reflection. The fall into sexual aberrations, which all human beings bear within themselves, stratified, can be recognized as a result of this reciprocal corruption of mental picturing and of willing and of their incapacity to meet again according to the original unity. It is the re-encounter that was no longer possible after the "fall," but that appears today as the possibility of the "I."

When the feeling of the re-encounter unites the two halves of the human couple and tends, by way of an autonomous impulse, to ascend toward its zone of sound-light, the stratification of the sexual involutions arises as the barrier that prevents the passage, or the knot that demands to be untied—so that up until yesterday only a sacrament like matrimony made the agreement of the couple possible, according to an internal protection relative to the control of corrupted impulses. By now, this protection has lost efficacy and meaning. Today, the stratification of the corrupted impulses ascends and asserts its rights on the human plane, not only by means of its psychology, but even through religious ethics.

The restitution of what was removed—namely, sacred love—demands a trans-humanizing and, nonetheless, rigorously individual action within the soul. It is the task of a feeling whose uncorrupted point, capable of resounding according to the ancient harmony, must be discovered within the soul. The flow of love, enlivened by its inner impulse, discovers the primordial element within itself. But to this end, it needs the spirit's other polarity, the impulse of knowledge, which gives it a way to insulate the sphere of stratification of the corrupted impulses from itself. One will see how the emergence of human self-consciousness has no other purpose.

The synthesis of the two polarities, thinking and willing, as a higher event of self-consciousness that restores the capacity of the ancient musicality to feeling, not only insulates the sphere of corrupt instincts, but it *knows* this sphere, as is not possible for any investigation of thinking inevitably conditioned by instincts. It knows this sphere according to a movement that, at each encountered stratum of sexual aberration, causes the equivalent transformative force from above to correspond, which thus becomes sacred love's force of ascension. Instinct does not become suppressed, but experienced at another level as a beneficial force.

Sacred love emerges as the unknown possibility in every human love, since it is its moment of elevation or of impersonality, capable of bearing to the couple the echo of extra-human bliss. It is a moment whose source is ignored by the couple and that, therefore, crossing over to (something) other, according to a development by now normal, loses its magical virtue. The couple can have a relative awareness of such a virtue when its magic has disappeared. The moment that magic is present, the forces of consciousness capable of taking it on usually do not exist. Such magic, nonetheless, can be taken on consciously and continued, brought towards its fulfillment, by means of a radical action of the conscious "I." It is a matter of understanding why self-consciousness arose and what its ultimate meaning is: certainly not to be subservient to physical life.

The magical ascension of feeling is the work of self-consciousness that seeks its inner source and, to this end, solicits a willing that reaches a deep zone. As we have mentioned, the rise of sacred love responds to a series of degrees of dynamic resolution of the various compounds of the deep stratification of sexual aberration. It is not a matter of sexual experiences but, rather, of operations that liberate through images. *Sexual aberration exerts its rule by means of a usurped imaginative power.* Self-consciousness has creative imagination as its true vehicle, namely the imagining that gradually reacquires its own element of life, in relation to becoming free of erotic impressions.

We can understand the sense of such a freeing action if we consider that the creative element lost by human imagining is in fact willing, or the current of life, which (as has been seen) having split from mental picturing because of longing, flows within the "lunar body."

Creative imagination is really an androgynous power. It is the beginning of a *conscious* synthesis of the forces of mental picturing and of willing. When the will flows into thinking, thanks to the discipline of concentration, the force of willing confers to thinking the power to free itself from the cerebral organ and to live according to its original current. It is the initial resurrection of the primordial solar current that permeates the Lunar Stone. Its initial movement leads it to encounter what opposes its true nature—the stratification of an erotic aberrant necessity. The ascension of a supernal life of feeling responds to each stratum that the current of imaginative life can encounter and resolve—a life of feeling that manifests as cosmic music resounding within the soul. The degree of bliss that can be experienced due to the utmost human 'falling-in-love,' is overcome by the ascension of such feeling.

Such an experience can only be realized as a metaphysical relationship of the two components of the human couple. It cannot be realized by the ascetic who walks alone. Ascetics who go alone can access higher levels of consciousness up to a limit, beyond which they cannot advance unless they recognize in *eros* the radical petition of nature, which poses a limit that evokes the virtue of sacred love. Any love turned toward the Divine, any emotional mysticism, or *bhakti*, any form of charity, affection or human compassion, is overcome by the impulse of sacred love—a sacred love that includes all of them and leads them to fulfillment, for which only those human beings as bearers of the "I" are prepared.

Human love can ascend to the Divine, or discover the Divine behind semblances, only if it overcomes the constraint that enslaves it to that degree of humanness, which consecrates the reification of the semblance. Such a level is not sex, but the stratification of the aberrant longings that has become physical nature. The asceticisms and mysticisms of the past did not require overcoming such constraint. The ascetics could establish a relation with the spiritual world by leaving aside the sphere of *eros*. In the age of the "I," this sphere posits itself as *the physical-metaphysical place that guards the keys to the reintegration.* Ascetics who proceed alone, at a given level, find that the human threshold coincides with the limit of the sphere of the human being's degradation. They cannot proceed any further without knowing the mystery of Isis-Sophia, which is the mystery of *eros'* redemption. For them, it is not only the experience of the inner woman but, above all, the encounter with the feminine being that impersonates it. The living presence of the woman bears the decisive element of the reintegration, as the power that it incarnates but does not realize except by means of the encounter.

The meaning of the "human state" is restored by sacred love, since this alone with its light can justify the presence of the categories of *eros*. Without such a justification, the phenomenology of sex, with its orgasms and its tensions, animal reproduction and everyday life of the human couple, is an event as obscure as it is tragically obtuse, which explains the catastrophes or the painful decadences that accompany it.

Each of the two (partners) is the bearer of a force that completes that of the other and that the other bears dormant within him or herself. Man has within him his own inner woman; woman has the inner man. Each spiritual development, being a continuous work of the synthesis of mental picturing and willing, is a movement of an androgynous reintegration. In that sense, man holds the keys of the androgynous restoration of woman, woman (holds the keys of the androgynous restoration) of man, in that the element of reintegration that each develops as an incorporeal value is incarnated in the other—namely, the celestial element in woman, the volitional-terrestrial element in man. The initiatic couple is able to enliven the incorporeal element, by means of which one completes the other. It is important to understand that it has nothing to do with a union according to reciprocal dependence but, rather, according to reciprocal liberation.

The encounter of the souls of the couple occurs according to the virtue of an androgynous archetypal entity, which lives simultaneously in the two, separated in soul of each by its subjection to individual-corporeal finiteness. The androgynous archetypal impulse, obtusely felt within the sensory sphere, leads the ordinary human couple to reunite, according to corporeal longing—in search of a bliss due to the momentary illusion of a self-transcendence, which, in the sexual act, is always at the point of manifesting but is quickly devoured by the lustful orgasm of the ego, aimed solely at feeling itself, at absorbing (according to an unconscious vampirism) the fluidic current of the other, in order to destroy it.

When the forces of self-consciousness awaken in us, we can fall into the error of believing that the ultimate aim of such self-consciousness is an earthly life more intense and more physically articulated. We can tend toward that organization of its dependence on the longing of life, which is the situation of the subversive-technological civilization. The absurdity of such an organization can be grasped, where it is thought that the forces of self-consciousness cannot be subjected to the lust for life, without changing and becoming destructive, given that their task is to inwardly penetrate life. The concrete purpose of self-consciousness is to realize the Principle of life—the Logos.

If self-consciousness draws from its own original forces, it discovers that the impediment to the realization of its own principle is the degradation of the human being bound by sex. Self-conscious human beings do not make the mistake of mystically avoiding the confrontation with sex, nor of undergoing it as an obvious human category. Instead, they notice the illicit power of such a category over consciousness and over the soul.

Self-conscious human beings discover what impedes them from realizing the life of the soul. They glimpse the splitting of thinking and of willing within the current of desire, which is a desire for each and every physical semblance and radically of sex. Their work is therefore a work of reconnecting the two faculties, which, at a given moment, demands fulfillment beyond the individual limit, since its purpose is to overcome what keeps the individual bound deeply. A new life of feeling is the sign of overcoming the individual limit. This new life is something more than a mystical event, since it is the radical activity of self-consciousness, which contains the possibility of every mystical experience. The rediscovery of the "inner woman" also becomes an outer event for man. The work of the self-conscious being and the direction of *karma* coincide.

The reunion of the couple becomes real both as an inner event, and as an outer accomplishment, or symbolic reality. The reunion is particularly the supra-sensory work of thinking and of willing. In order for this reunion to be brought to fruition, it must resurrect hearing, as a measure of the audibility of the celestial sound. Ascetics who can listen to this celestial sound know the mystery of Isis-Sophia, from which they receive the original union's force of restoration—the hidden sense of Androgyny.

The reunion of the couple, as the conscious resurrection of the Earth's primordial virtue, cannot but be opposed by the powers that dominate us via the past, or that of the Earth which is dead. It cannot but confront tragic trials, nevertheless having against it what appears as an ethical or legalistic or discursive value on Earth—*the immense power of the conventional.*

5.

THE RECONQUEST OF THE ORIGINAL ACCORD

We can say that the spiritual force that operated at the beginning can potentially be gathered in the current function of the "I." This force now acts within the "I" as the very power by means of which the "I" estranged itself from it, in order to be autonomous. The meaning of the birth of the "I" is the adherence of the spirit to the sensible categories, up to an identity that tends to annihilate it. At the present time, the annihilation reaches such a point, that it requires the "I" to rediscover its identity with itself. This, in short, is the sense of the *physical* experience of the "I," which unfolds until excluding (yet also arousing) its reality, which is *metaphysical.*

From a cosmological point of view, we can say that the "I" identifies with the categories of minerality, or with the dominion of the Serpent, in that the Serpent's domineering forces and the ordering forces of the Cosmos, at a given moment, emerge as the foundation of self-consciousness, there, where we are unaffected by the Serpent, *in an area of total independence, where we truly exist, but unknowingly.* The radical supra-sensory essence allows us to identify with minerality and lose ourselves within the sensory, until we deny our own supra-sensory being.

We can understand how the "I" is able to carry out the task of realizing its true nature by negating what it is, given that it is identified with sensory nature. We have seen how such an identification is bound in the depths by longing and by sex. *The "I" is unaware of the superhuman power of its movement of identity, obtusely aimed at the world of semblances.* The sense of its reintegration is that it can turn such power toward what is real and permanent, beyond semblance. In the "I," we can recognize, as hidden, the force capable of reacquiring the dominion of *light* lost by the original couple, and the dominion of *life* lost by the androgynous being that precedes it.

Through the unconscious identification with the world of semblances, the polarity of the manifestation of the "I" in the sensory sphere emerges opposite to that of its original force. Sex is one with the power that prohibits the communion of the "I" with its own essence. But such power belongs to the "I." Therefore, the undertaking of discovering the "I" consists in freeing the transcendent element within the dominion of sex.

The myth of the origins highlights the sense of the profound relationship between self-consciousness and sex. The radical willing by means of which we adhere to sensory matter is the Spirit's original force diverted. We are placed in a position to divert it toward sensory *appearing,* that is, toward the negation of the Spirit, because from such a diversion we have the possibility of autonomy. Autonomy manifests as opposition to the Spirit, because of the telluric-lunar forces that have brought it about. Such forces remain within human nature to the extent that human autonomy unknowingly appeals to them. By means of sex, they simultaneously hold the constraint of self-consciousness and the expression of autonomy solely as a function of the craving for the sensory (realm)—egoism.

Today that opposition has exhausted its purpose. Yet, we persist in this opposition without perceiving it. The opposition can be overcome by the forces of life and of sound, or of the solar Logos, which initially ruled the lower currents of the Earth. These forces of life and of sound continue to overcome the lunar darkness, that is, the radical resistance of physical matter, to continuously make possible the reproductive act and the birth of a new human being in the maternal womb. Today, self-consciousness has the task of reconnecting with these forces, *to avoid the forming of a sub-human generation, only physically evolved.*

The consciousness of the original couple was harmonically correlated with the Powers of life and of sound, by means of its own forces of light. It allowed them to carry out their work, receiving from them a beatific *life of light*. The light of consciousness was connected to the powers of sound through the current of life. The union of their bodies took place according to a pure spontaneity—of the light's life— governed by the highest forces of the Logos, with respect to which human beings were in a state of deep sleep. We went awakening self-consciousness as the correlation of our forces of light with the sensory (sphere), outside the agreement with life and with sound. Thus, there arose within us a longing for the physical appearance of the other (partner), no longer seen as an inner being but, rather, as a sensory form—the light's shadow.

Being awake by means of egoic consciousness makes us lose the pure correlation, which we were once able to have with the forces of the Word operating in the sexual act. The connection with these (forces) becomes impure, insofar as it occurs according to *the longing for a form* that—in being exclusively valid as a sensory form—is the symbol of when the forces of lower darkness manage to have the upper hand over us. In fact, because of this upper hand, we initially lose the androgynous power, and then the angelic correlation of the original couple. It is the time of the Serpent.

The Serpent symbolizes the degradation of the original force and the level from which this (force) must be resurrected. From the moment of the degradation, each sexual pleasure would be an inverted aspect of supra-human blessedness. Each human being would, however, seek, by means of their soul's forces, the soul of the other (partner) in bodily appearance. Sexual joy would give them the fleeting sensation of rediscovering an original good but, inevitably, they would always be disappointed.

Pleasure continuously disappointed, but that draws us according to the longing continuously rekindled, leads us to seek—beyond the form of fulfillment that has become normal— what (because of addiction and delusion) we believe is hidden in other forms. Each sexual perversion is the illusory play of longing that leads us to seek, in additional ways of bodily *eros*, something that inevitably escapes us, because it belongs to the soul and not to corporeality. The series of sexual perversions is the dominion of the inverse force, or the force of the Serpent, constitutionally present in all living beings, as a radical stamp that imprints the whole of earthly nature, involving (through human prevarication) the animal world and, in part, that of the plant.

The degradation of *eros* in accordance with the current of longing is the inevitable result of the spirit's descent into corporeality, right down to sensory consciousness. From this, as we have seen, self-consciousness arises, which in the merely rational form is the human being's recent conquest. Therefore, the human being's re-ascension is essentially seen as a resolution of the strata of that sexual degradation, which is the price of self-consciousness. Self-consciousness cannot be limited to being a rational fact. Other levels of being must incarnate it, so that it can be a living reality and not a mere dialectical phenomenon.

The re-ascension to our original status cannot but find itself before the stratified barrier of sexual degradation. *To each awakening of the original spiritual faculty, there responds as counterpoint a degree of the corruption of eros.* The task of the Grail disciples is not the traditional one, namely to *ascetically* detach themselves from the category of the senses, or to let this category be ruled *sacredly* by a ritualistic wisdom transcendent to them but, rather, to proceed to the gradual resolution of each stratum by means of an inner alchemy. Their initial task is to perceive inwardly the bonds that bring about degradation within the soul. Such perception becomes the vehicle of the forces of Redemption. Today, the "I" has within it the possibility of becoming aware of the meaning of its own history and of the relationship that binds its inner life to an image of the body and of the physical world, assumed as real to the extent that they are bereft of their living content.

Today, through the activity of the consciousness soul, we can—insofar as we are free—codify our state of dependence on the sensory to the point of absurdity, by making use of science, to the extent that this (science) is oblivious of its own fundamental cognitive process. But in such a manner, we will betray our own spiritual nature definitively and lose the opportunity of the "I," whose purpose is to restore the original magic-solar nature by recovering the stages that lead to it—namely, stages along which we have descended, through sexual alienation, down to the present-day rational-sensory condition.

The movement of self-awareness conceals within it the vital lymph of the intact force of the "I." Thanks to the presence of this intact force, the "I" can call on itself for the secret of its profound nature and the path of re-ascension; it can move according to a clear choice and a pure decision of the will.

The undertaking, obscured by the symbolism of the Grail, leads us to recognize the Serpent's power within the soul. Parsifal cannot do anything to redeem the Grail, before recognizing the lower magic of Chastel Marveil, subtly operating in him as well. The recognition of the serpentine power, as the human being's highest *animadversio* (observation), is already the conquering force acting within the soul—namely, the force of the Logos. From it the vision of the task arises, for which the undertaking can be realized. The task, intuited and assumed, turns out to be an undertaking for the resolution of *eros*, involving a new experience of the human couple's relationship. The two are at the point of closing a long cycle of dispersion; therefore, they find each other.

The discovery demands a state of deep concentration of the soul's faculties and *the ultimate decision of dedication*. A clear decisive experience of the Spirit presents itself. For the seeker capable of such a decision, there is the other being of the original accord that awaits. But it is man who must be ready. It can be said that woman is virtually ready. (It is) a poetic undertaking, an undertaking of the most immaterial love, an ideal that appears unrelated to the brute *dynamis* of daily reality and to the empire of the sensory world, equipped with its technology, with its ethics and with its mysticism. And yet, it is a concrete undertaking of knowledge and power. It is the most practical undertaking, the true human undertaking; (this undertaking is the) bearer of the force that alone can give humanity a new impulse. It is not simple mystical love, *bhakti,* the wonder of the Indian spirit, the devotion of the Christian saints or of Islamic ascetics, but something more essential and dynamic, that *can only now be born on Earth*—namely, sacred love.

The task is to discover the currents of the light and the life lost in a sexual experience governed by desire. Such a control can be contemplated, and in contemplation it can be dissolved. In the *embrace* that barely unites the bodies, because it moves from hearts—it being a greeting of the soul's encounter or outpouring with the soul—the abandonment that is complete according to the demand of the heart, is the initial sign of the flow of light.

It is the symbol of a *union that must not be betrayed.* It is the embrace in which the spinal cord, or the spine, participates, but not sex. The form of the spinal column is the form of the Dragon or the Serpent. In the pure embrace, as an encounter of soul to soul, the Serpent begins to be enchanted by a music no longer heard. It then tends to retreat into itself, leaving the path of the *heart* free.

Resistance to this embrace or the incapacity of a complete abandonment immune from craving, is a sign of rejecting the light. The embrace, as a momentary communion of the heart, is the slightest ecstasy that ignores desire, rising from the opposite of desire—self-devotion. If bodily desire awakens, this is the sign of a self-giving that is still incomplete—a persistent refusal of the light. The refusal is, however, the profound tendency of the "lunar body," the area of the Serpent's dominion, capable of providing every emotion and exaltation except self-giving. The measure of independence from such a dominion is the embrace, as an encounter of the soul, in which the light-life current that corresponds to self-abandonment is objectively experienced.

The self-giving of Eastern and Western mysticisms cannot summon the strength to transcend the zone of the Serpent since it lacks the element of the arid metallic light of abstract or reflected thought, where the soul's total abandonment is realized as a death, from which alone the light's resurrection is possible. Therefore, the soul's secret relationship—as the life-light of Isis-Sophia—to the androgynous power of the "I" is missing.

From the perception of this death of dialectical, formal rational thought, the knowledge of a re-lighting of the life-light, that is not the vivification of the reflected light, is possible. The impulse of a new mysticism is needed, which bears in itself the force of all ancient mysticisms, and moreover a new element in the world, a *total and heroic* element, capable of overcoming the limit, which exists only now in its totality and inevitability. Each past spiritual doctrine can be seen as a gift that flows across a threshold still subsisting within the limit line. Now each threshold is closed; the limit rules in its entirety. Therefore, beyond the squalor of such a modern condition, a willful self-annihilation is possible, as a conscious act.

Overcoming the limit is the task of self-consciousness,

which, only today, can positively bring about willful self-giving, or the total annihilation of its own ephemeral form. It can arouse that offering of the seat of feeling, or the seat of rhythms, where there is no longer a need to fight instinctively and passionately, because the death of thinking has created a void, *the nothingness of ancient feeling,* in which the light of life, new and sublime, shines through. In alchemical language, we can say that profound soul forces cross over from the experience of the transcendent nature of *water* (Moon) to that of the transcendent nature of *air* (Sun). It is passing from the lower waters to the higher waters, the beginning of the *Operatio Solis,* or Grand Opera. Water is transformed into air, in that the forces of light and sound operate as the *fire* that warms the Earth. The water contained in the earth ascends from the depths, again becoming the original "air of projection." Self-giving can be experienced in the moment of the embrace, but also evoked in memory of this (embrace). However, there is the possibility that the willing of man's heart arouses the angelic core of the woman's soul, which, in turn, emerges as a *reference* of a devotion, as vast as it is powerful, which sums up all the forces of the ego, insofar as it utilizes within the soul the identical channel by means of which willing normally becomes the longing of the ego.

Along these lines, the possibility of opening up to the etheric current continuously nourished by the blood, as the heart's power of light, gives itself to both (man and woman). The presence of the Logos in the human heart, normally opposed by the etheric mental current, is allowed to ascend as an individual virtue. The profound donation to which we have referred is possible insofar as the qualitative change of the cerebral mental current has been prepared, by means of a discipline capable of reaching the intact original *dynamis* of thinking. Which is to say, the current of the light of thinking gathers within itself the heart's flowing ether, so that it can become, in the vehicle of the sound-life forces, the conscious will of self-offering.

At this point, one can speak of a *Christic ataraxia,* as an invulnerability, or elusiveness, that begins to reign in the area of the Serpent. This area is not the place of sex, but the area of the cerebral organ and the spinal cord. The experience of a Christic ataraxia, as the soul's complete estrangement from the nervous system, is understandable, provided that the right meaning is given to this expression, of ceasing to depend on habitual reactions which, as such, are the movements of desire and of the ego—so that one comes to realize, without predetermination, the image: "Not I, but the Christ in me." It is a realization that is equivalent to that of a deep calm, of the capacity to endure any adversity, to contemplate any catastrophe or human tragedy, without being minimally changed by it; receiving, penetrating everything with liberating consciousness, thanks to an imperturbability that is not insensitivity, but the acceptance of the being as it is, insofar as one is at the center of such a being. One cooperates in the process of redeeming the world according to the correlation of sacred love—the true love for the world.

The correlation, therefore, is not a reference to anything but its original element. Meanwhile, in ordinary love, the correlation is reciprocal dependence. Sacred love is the synthesis of liberated individualities. The discovery of the Higher "I" is the free "I"'s overcoming of itself: self-giving to the point of a zero, or to a void, or to an annihilation of what is valid as earthly appearing. In this moment of annihilation, the unlimited gift flows, because the "I" is filled with its ancient life. However little it appears to ordinary observation, such a power of self-giving is experienced in the embrace as a greeting of a pure encounter since it is the act of the "I," which in a movement finds its own nature symbolically realized. Within feeling, the identity with the other, mediated by the etheric body, realizes for split-seconds its own superhuman nature. The gesture actualizes, by means of the soul's limbs, the encounter of the fluidic currents of the Androgyny.

In the inability to abandon ourselves to this embrace or to abandon ourselves unto to our very roots, we can receive within ourselves what refuses the Logos—the real impediment to spiritual development. We can recognize the fear of having to follow the Spirit, or the aversion to the Spirit, which is to say, the subjugation to the Serpent—namely, the fear of becoming lost.

The physical-metaphysical embrace alluded to here is not the sexual act, but in its simplicity, it is the extent of disentanglement of the radical force of sex, since the identical power of one's self-abandonment proper to the sexual act is realized as an abandonment to the pure movement of the soul. It is the same force, inverted, insofar as it is reconnected to its own principle. This movement is recognized as the identical current of life that obtusely sinks into sex and that can free itself in the sexual act, if it can be continued, all the way to its radical nature, according to the impulse from which it moves—namely, all the way to the depths where it is the substance of the *Operatio Solare.*

You may recall that the essential nature of the "I" is to identify with everything by remaining unchanged in itself, according to a unifying power that does not undergo duality. The "I"'s path of awareness is essentially acquiring this power of inalterability in the identity with the other. The total giving of oneself in the sexual act is an obscure form, or a sensual alteration, of the "I"'s power of identity with the world—the original androgynous power degraded. Self-giving could once again become an ordinary event, if it takes place according to the real nature of the "I." In fact, the powers of sound and of life, which primordially operated in sex, uncontaminated by longing, now pass through the "I." They are powers within the "I," unknown to reflected consciousness. Self-consciousness bears within itself the possibility of the relationship that the soul of primordial human beings had with sex, in that it essentially identified itself with the forces of sound and of life that operated there. Self-consciousness is itself woven of such forces.

Self-giving would again become the vehicle of the original identity, if developed according to the real nature of the "I," namely according to its proper seat, the soul's incorporeal sphere, as it occurs in the pure embrace—that is, the relationship being lifted from the sphere of *water* to that of *air*. Self-giving can be evoked and imaginatively perceived. With respect to it, self-alienation imposed from outside by sexual necessity is felt as a radical self-giving that has been altered. Self-giving begins to be experienced with equal radicalness as a profound tendency of the will, reconnected to the sphere of *fire*, that demands an everyday ritualistic enlivening—its mood is calmness without any support.

The deep calm in the resurrected current of the will, which bears within itself the power usually alienated in the delirium of sexual pleasure, becomes known. Such delirium is always a *swooning of the will.* The will rises up through an impulse that it draws from the depths of itself, since it is original to it—the current of a cosmic will. This normally flows in the movement of the limbs, but it becomes unnatural and is paralyzed in the sexual sphere, according to a darkening that impedes the soul from beholding its own deprivation of life and the consequent inversion of its force.

In reality, what the soul lacks is life. Because of this profound deprivation (*eros* normally being one with consciousness all the way to its source, so that there is no human act that does not have the mark of longing), the possibility of a will that follows the reverse path can only be realized in a donation of identical radicality and depth. This is the real movement of the "I," the ascent of sacred love—the initial restoration of life.

6.

THE POWER OF LIGHT AND OF FIRE. KUNDALINI

The product of the inverse force, or of the spirit that becomes longing, is reflected thought—the inversion of the light that, becoming knowledge, corresponds to truth only with regards to the weight and the measurement of things, namely to their appearing.

To re-ascend from reflected thought to its light, that is, from semblance to reality, means to retrace the path of egoism and of longing backwards. We can understand how such a task, despite the linearity of its logic, has no longer been understood, particularly by those who are able to speculatively codify the forms of semblance and of longing on the reflected plane. But there is no human problem that does not refer to such a task.

To re-ascend from reflection to the light means to rediscover a cosmic current of life, of unlimited depth, that limits itself within the human soul by being reflected in the cerebral organ as thought. This life of light, in its impersonality, is the fabric of human love. Those of us who follow the path of Initiation, by discovering the living light of thought, perceive its arising from the heart's fluidic center and can recognize the work's completion in the possibility of actualizing the identity with such a center. We glimpse the path of sacred love as overcoming the barrier between the life of the light, which we receive as a current of liberated thinking and the source of such life, which is the heart. The barrier is sex.

The distinction between the light of life of thinking and the source of its force, which one recognizes in the heart, is fundamental. The life of the light is connected with the heart, where it hides a deeper force—the cosmic current of the higher "I." If the passage from the reflection to the light can be alchemically indicated as a passage from the "inferior waters" to the "superior waters," the elevation from the light to the life of the light can be said to correspond to the elevation of vision from the nature of *water* to that of *air*. Analogously, to connect oneself to the source of the heart forces means achieving identity with the transcendent nature of *fire*. For this reason, tantric texts speak of the "fire" of *kundalini*.

Any power of "fire" that we naturally have at our disposal is impure, be it the warmth of thinking, of feeling and of the will. In any case, it has to do with a warmth of longing, whose path leads back to sex, not because the original fire is hidden there but, rather, because the process of its alteration is realized in sex. The key to the alteration lies outside of sex. The power of sex upon the soul is the result of the alteration of the force, which is perpetrated in the *a-sexual zones* of the soul.

The central fire of *kundalini* does not sleep safeguarded by sex. On the contrary, the transcendent power of sex sleeps safeguarded by the power of its alteration; the location of its intact essence is the depths of the heart. The mental (sphere's) opposition to the heart's etheric current makes the force's alteration possible. The wound of Amfortas cannot be cured of this alteration's poison. From sex, the profound consequence of the alteration arrives as an impure fire, the potential matter of solar magic for whoever knows the key of the alteration obscured in the symbolism of the Grail, in the symbols of the Spear and the Cup, which allude to the bravery of Parsifal due to the restoration of the Light's Principle. Such a restoration is realized through the purification of the impure fire: not of sex, but of the conscious will.

Investigators who through sex tend to open up to this impure fire begin from the naïve assumption that they are able to find its source here: hence the various attempts of sexual magic. The misunderstanding of such attempts consists in soliciting from sex subtle forces that, by means of the relationship implicit to the solicitation, enslave the person who opens up to them even more. They constitute the lower etheric-astral element that normally conveys the synthesis of the solar-lunar currents needed for the sexual act. Such a synthesis, however, is the work of a more elevated force, which escapes non-supra-sensory perception and, therefore, any operation conducted by means of physical sensations. The force manifests as the fire of *kundalini*, but its center is the heart.

In reality, the Serpent is not the fire of *kundalini*, but the symbol of its sexual *facies,* with respect to human beings possessed by longing. The serpentine power is the power of longing, namely a power already inverted. It is power insofar as it rules human beings, not insofar as it is a power in itself. It dominates those human beings who believe that they need to strive toward it and not toward the force, whose *perception it impedes.* The Serpent is not the original force but, rather, the symbol of the altered force, which, as such—or, with its power of alteration—can be aroused and magically taken on. Here, the contradiction of erotic magic is gathered. Those who take on the altered force cannot control it, because such force manifests to them in line with their subjugation to longing. They are controlled by it. The Serpent obeys only the force that has subjugated it and has delimited its power. Such a force springs from the center of the heart. It can be experienced thanks to a type of inner action alluded to in the series of moments of the Grail's undertaking.

Those of us who pursue the path of the Grail, at a given moment, find the power of the Serpent opposite us, but we discover that such power is carried out from the sexual sphere, since initially we are subjected to it outside this sphere, by opposing the heart's original virtue (the mighty dominator of the Serpent) via the forces of the serpentine fire—of the senses, of the instincts, and of the passions.

If the path toward the heart passes through thinking—to the extent that thinking is capable of opening up to its own inner light—the assumption of the power of *eros* passes through the heart. The power that dominates sex is drawn from the center of the heart, but once the experience of sex is confronted with such power, the impulse that frees itself from it leads back to the heart.

The light of thinking becomes the life of the light. If this life of the light unites with the wellspring of the heart, one prepares to receive within oneself the original adamantine element. Ascetics of the Grail understand the task that awaits them at such a point, to the extent that, by tending toward the adamantine element, they find the path barred by the Serpent's power. In reality, *the Serpent's power bars the path toward the source of the heart, because from such a source flows the force that subjugates it.* Those who arrive at the Threshold of the Spiritual World learn that crossing the Threshold and radically confronting the force of *eros* are an identical task.

It has become clear how, at this point, the subsequent path is not the magic of sex but, rather, the path of sacred love. The current of the light of thinking is continued in the life of the light. This life of the light is born cold in its incorporeal purity. It demands not to be grasped by the warmth of the senses, so that it can restore metaphysical warm to the senses. Thus, it becomes the power of resurrection of feeling, which puts an end to the deception of Lucifer, of the reflected light, of fluctuating and deceptive feelings.

The life of the light follows the path of the Serpent within the current of *kundalini*. In this way, it is imbued with a warmth that is not derived from the senses, in that it has the coldness of the Serpent's blood and the power of the original warmth. *The Serpent's secret is cold blood, whose virtue we have lost.* On the Grail path, the soul does not have to draw warmth from the sphere of the senses. The senses ask it for the life of which the mental (sphere) deprives them. By virtue of sacred love, the soul retraces the inversion of the light within the sensory, and experiences the life of the light, until finding the pure power of fire.

Self-consciousness has the task of retracing the inversion of the light. Ascetics can arrive at the consecration of themselves to the extent that they will according to the forces of the overturned ego. The absoluteness that characterizes the ego's self-willing in the physical world becomes the spirit's channel. The overturning of the ego's forces is the Serpent's movement according to forces, which, from the very beginning, make use of its power for human reproduction on the animal plane. Unknown to us and nevertheless operating in the sexual act, such forces, by acting, normally exclude all human control, because our willing is subjected to the Serpent's enchantment. We adhere sleepily to the sexual sphere, by means of longing and pleasure.

As mentioned above, disengagement from the power of the

Serpent begins as a passage from reflected thought to living thinking. If it is to be radically realized, it demands a new life of feeling. This (new life) identifies with the experience of sacred love. The task is determined by the need to integrate elements of the soul's life, which can be reawakened in relation to the petition of the original synthesis, from which arises the need for the other half of the human couple to cooperate. Nevertheless, the pairing thus reconstituted moves from a decision prepared in the extra-temporal sphere, according to an agreement whose origin is superhuman. The superhuman element must return to the human being.

There is no movement of human love that is not contaminated by the Serpent. Sacred love, incapable of not moving within the sphere of such contamination, begins by opposing this contamination with the force of devotion inherent in the meditation concerning the figure of light of the other. Later, beyond the figure of light, the investigator gathers the adamantine archetype as the principle itself of the light, more deeply active in the beloved, right down to their corporeal being. The perception of this archetype is reciprocal, and it is the sign of independence from the contamination.

We can turn to the angelic-binomial being, with the forces that dominate the Serpent, insofar as we discover that the ultimate aim of that longing—for which we are subjected to the play of the Serpent—actually belongs to an area of the soul where the Serpent is powerless. We must discover this ancient deception. The sign of sacred love arising in us is the perception of such areas. We can overcome the millennial contradiction within us if we become conscious of that part of the soul with respect to which we are immersed during sleep, but to which we appeal through conscious thinking.

The redemption of thinking and the flow of sacred love have the same movement. There, the pure forces of light and of life coincide. The forces of light are lost in the visible world, if what lies at the origin of the light does not lead them back to the light's function before the advent of the Serpent, because, truly, in the beginning was the Logos, or the primordial power of sound. Today, after the millennial travail of philosophizing, whereby the Logos obscurely emerges in the content, thinking contains a power of light, which still remains unknown to it, namely the power of liberating the soul from the dominion of Lucifer, if it can grasp within itself the light's movement by means of which it thinks—the life of the light. It is a life with respect to which it, as dialectical thought, is dormant; (it is) awake only through illusory sensory contents and corresponding abstractions—the deceptive reflection of the light.

The life of the light begins in the movement-light of thinking; the life of the light is the ethereal vestment of sacred love, by virtue of which we encounter within us the power of redemption from the Serpent's contamination. We find intact within us the magical forces of the origins that once halted the Serpent. The intervention of the Redeemer restored them as the germ of a Resurrection, which is a faculty of ours to implement. Such a germ of light barely surfaces in the etheric or non-dialectical moment of the concept. It can be awakened though the enlivening of the concept until it identifies with the current of sacred love, where it is the continuity of the Resurrection, which carries out each resurrection in those of us who at this point know how to recognize and experience our own death, the ordinary condition of the soul devoid of the life of the light. We exhaust death. Beyond an area called the Field of Death, each component (of the) human couple experiences love as a resurrection of a celestial accord, which *can never again fail* and which operates in the world as the model of the definitive uniqueness of the union. It is sacred love, the love of the rediscovered Isis-Sophia, whose symbol is the Virgin, crowned with stars, upright on the crescent of the Moon, with her feet on the head of the Ancient Adversary.

The human limit that is thus overcome is the limit of reflected thought, which theoreticians of the spirit aspire to overcome, even seeking it in their own interiority; seeking it everywhere, except within the thinking by means of which they think, because it is the thinking that is most immediate to them, too dear, too much at one with their egoic nature, for them to be able to detach from it. It is thinking that is one with mineral semblance, with the tangible world, just as the serpent is one with the earth upon which it slithers. Reflected thought is the most difficult limit to perceive, even when it is theoretically recognized. Its overcoming in fact seems to be a simple event of thinking but, in reality, it is an event of the whole soul, which is on the verge of seeing its ancient bondage to appearance, to longing, to fear, to the Earth's idols, dissolve. For this reason, we must say that such an overcoming is not only a volitional act of thinking, but, at the same time, a total and heroic surge of the whole soul.

The moment of freed thinking is the moment of decision of a level from which a more-than-human force erupts within us, a more radical power, which cannot come from the human being, (a power) to which the human being is normally closed off and resists because of the congenital fear of knowing it—a power that alone can change the human, a force that is before and at the origin of the human, a higher virtue that does not need effort to be what it is.

The will of this moment is a turbine of force that overwhelms the mediocrity of the existential hypocrisy of the everyday play of semblances—a breeze, or a breath of the peaks, a dizzying immobility and a swiftness of presence. It is a will that can be willed only by overcoming the soul's apparent death, through a sublime self-willing beyond the dialectical consumption of consciousness, by profoundly offering itself *to the being that bears, intact, the etheric jewel* of eternity to the celestial living creature, which can change it into the warmth of life through a gift (that is) itself of a superhuman type—namely sacred love, the restorer of love in the world.

We have in self-conscious willing a primordial power of decision. We can open the passage within ourselves to the powers of sound and of life that are at the origin. The Power of the Word that is at the Beginning of life and of humanity, can, thanks to an act of free will, flow into humanity. Lining up against this free act are the powers that have the task of preventing the emergence of sacred love as a force of human redemption.

The cosmic need for the Seat of the Mysteries of the new times to be formed on Earth requires, above all, that *more Solis** begin the rite of sacred love. A fabric of golden light is inserted into the light of the world as a rekindling force of the human intellect. The work of the *initiatic couple* takes place on the

---

*   Solar will (way/will of the sun)

supra-mental plane where the archetypes of human events are in progress. Therefore, each variation of the ritual is reflected on the earthly plane as a power of destiny.

The Seat of the Mysteries is edified by the light of life and by the warmth of consecration, interwoven as a spatial reality, in which one can penetrate and exist. Its structure is erected by the dedication and sacrifice of the couple who, day by day, hour by hour, minute by minute, thought by thought, elaborate the redeeming lymph of the Earth—sacred love.

However extraneous to the world scene and to spiritual practice it may seem, the creation of such a sacred environment is the most positive activity regarding the objective problems of the Earth. If, despite the systematic alienation of the forces in the mechanism and in the cult of instinctiveness, our practical behavior does not burst into self-destruction, this is due to the everyday ritual of those working to build the new Seat of the Mysteries. Each day, this work pits the powers of liberation against the persistence of the struggle of longings and of hatred in an ethical-social guise. It evokes the life of the light and the fire of pure willing, the forces of recollection and silence, according to a ritual whose purpose is to unite with the Seat of the Mysteries the individualities of the new times called to the undertaking of the Grail and yet unaware of their calling.

The power of the Serpent of *kundalini* is indeed the power of the original fire, but strong in its alteration. As such, it bars our passage towards *the pure power of fire.* The alteration regards the human being, not the Serpent. Humans ruled by the Serpent cannot grasp the power of the Serpent; they cannot turn to it to possess the power whose alteration is maintained by this Serpent. Asking the Serpent for power is a movement of the power's deprivation—an ulterior form of deception.

The deprivation does not regard the Serpent, even if the Serpent is its symbol. It regards us as humans. We lost the Ancient Mysteries for not having known how to use thinking—a consequence of the deprivation—in the service of true know-ledge, which is to penetrate the secret meaning of the deprivation. The new Seat of the Mysteries is erected so that the knowledge of that secret can be restored and human beings can again operate according to their real life—the life of the light. The couple was separated so that, as a result of their desire to come together, the force of sacred love—the Life of the light that will defeat earthly darkness—can be born on Earth.

7.

THE METAPHYSICAL CIRCUIT OF THE FORCE

Those of us who, freed from a series of earthly ties, have taken life to its extreme, compelling it to stand before itself, in nude and irreversible contrast, through an act of absolute will, or self-giving, or consecration, may have come to the moment of our journey where we are allowed to encounter on Earth the being of sacred love, the *other* by which to rebuild the Mystery, which is not a rebuilding but, rather, a rediscovery of something that had been forgotten.

We see this being come to meet us as an *angel of devotion*, arousing our own devotion, while we bear to it the *knowledge* that demands to be elevated from the human level to the angelic level. Both will know that sacred love cannot take root on Earth if it does not overcome the Earth's limit, which for them is also the secret of earthly experience and of the Threshold of the Spiritual World.

The virtue of sacred love operates within the soul simultaneously on both sides of the Threshold. To carry it out in an area of the conscious soul means to spark its emergence beyond the "higher darkness," where its corresponding transcendence lives. For each person, the real image of the other exists in this zone as an *adamantine archetype* that indicates the androgynous path of reintegration.

The possibility of contemplating this archetype of the other, beyond the everyday figure, even the most idealized, is a sign of the ascent of sacred love, but simultaneously the ritualistic work that, daily, demands the impulse of its ascending moment, since it is the contemplation of the greatest human Mystery. The archetype is one for both, but *for each one, it assumes the image of the other.* The power of love arises from contemplating such a Mystery, which also possesses the meaning of the real birth of the "I." The Higher "I" can arise in us by being able to give itself to something that it is not, but with which it manages to identify until negating itself. It is the experience of self-transcendence that gives Parsifal a way to understand, beyond doubt and rebellion, the sacred content of the Grail.

Near the Threshold of the Spiritual World, both attain magical certainty. Human love, the love that ordinarily connects two beings, from the soul to the body, does not come from the body. It does not come from the psyche bound to the body, but from the spirit. It comes from the uncontaminated incorporeal areas, outside of consciousness and of the psyche. An erotic attraction, even the most sensual, in effect, does not come from the body. Love, as an impulse that reunifies the couple, does not originate from sex. Instead, the attraction between the sexes is a lower reflection of the love that springs from an incorporeal source. Certainly, the lower reflection can arrive at an automatism of its own, which can give the illusion of a process founded on corporeality.

The real circuit of the force that manifests as *eros*, by not belonging to sex but to the soul and, even more radically, to remote regions of the spirit, effectively undergoes an inversion in sex. For this reason, it manifests as *eros.* The misunderstanding of contemporary science and of spiritualistic doctrines that contemplate methods of sexual initiations is to believe that sex holds the key to the force. In reality, what appears as *eros* is the inversion of the force. However, it is not sex that holds the key to the inversion but, rather, the relationship of the mental (sphere) with the nervous system and, particularly, with the cerebral organ. The force of *eros*—which manifests in the most obscure forms of longing and gradually seems to become spiritualized as it presents itself as a correlation of the soul—does not arise from corporeality. It is not an emanation of sex. Instead, it is the polarity opposite to corporeality and to sex. It irradiates within us from a mysterious source that we cannot conceive. Nonetheless, the site of its alteration and, thus, of its restoration is the human mental (sphere).

Humans in love, those of us who, as they say, are "smitten," are effectively permeated for a relatively short time by supernatural forces, which are of the same order as those operating in a mystical *raptus,* namely extra-conscious forces, capable of beatifying us, temporarily making another being out of each one of us. Possessed by such forces, we feel dis-individualized, capable of (making) any sacrifice for our beloved. We can arrive at a self-giving that transcends the usual limit. It is a moment where, through love, we can overcome ourselves, defeat our own *ego*, feel ready for any action demanding courage, self-forgetfulness, that is offered unconditionally. *But it is not sex; it is the spirit*—the spirit, however, not known and that therefore, not known, not received according to the conditions that it requires, according to a *noesis* through which the soul can allow itself to be illuminated by this spirit. Unnoticed, this spirit disappears, returns to its cosmic circuit since we, the enamored, believe we recognize it where it is not, in corporeal sensation, in the form of the other, in sex—there, where its force is inverted.

The misunderstanding where we believe to find in sex the primal force that presents itself as *eros*, is not detected by any present esoteric investigation. In effect, the problem occurs in its complexity in current times, insofar as the ancient voices, suggestions and rules fall silent—(ancient voices, etc.) which, in spite of everything, even recently related *eros* to a higher order and to the Mystery: through communions of forces, rather than through processes of knowledge.

The path of knowledge belongs to the present age, but it, too, is barred by the correlative dialectics. Today, we believe that we can rationally confront the problem whose content is entirely extra-rational and, in an esoteric-spiritualistic center, we are not able to overcome the ambiguity of sexual magic. Not that this is impossible. For now, what effectively turns out to be impossible is the awareness of the forces that need to awaken so that such magic can be achieved. Erotic magic—of the kind that is most worthy of consideration today—believes that it can offer a method to experientially catch unawares the primordial hidden force within sex, by imparting the insertion of its *dynamis* into the spontaneous process through a predisposed volitional act. In the experimenter, such magic presupposes the capacity to perceive the *dynamis*—which is supra-sensory—by naively identifying it with its sensory repercussion, that is, with erotic sensation. The *primal* force cannot be subjected to such tricks. To reveal itself and to flow, it needs to be aroused by an element that is itself primal, of a superhuman order, which, if present, would not need the sexual act to awaken the force, but would encounter it independently of this (act). Consequently, it could experience sex magically, not in order to take possession of a force that it does not need but, rather, to re-consecrate the act of human generation, so that a human type, free from the stain of lustful egoity, can be born.

To unfold, the etheric *dynamis* of *eros* needs to be opposed by an element independent of the sexual current, namely an inner principle, capable of encountering it outside of its *maya,* that is, outside of the mental process, which makes it appear in the guise of pleasure and complete in its physicality until it functions as a sensory transcendence. In effect, the force is transcendent, but as supra-sensory. The inner principle that can encounter it must therefore be simultaneously mental and supra-sensory. It is the thinking capable of freeing itself from the cerebral organ and, thus, of actualizing the non-inverted force. As long as it is inverted, the force operates, ungraspable, all the way to the physical phenomenology. Yet, the ordinary human being does not even penetrate into this (phenomenology), gathering from it only the repercussions that interest the "body of longing," or the lower astral body, which, in turn, dignifies its dependence by means of inner or intellectual or scientific expressions. Lustful sensations take excessive hold of us (as ordinary individuals), up to levels we do not suspect, so that we, detached, can re-ascend from them to the real physical phenomenon—from which alone re-ascension to the metaphysical is possible.

The original vital body of the human being can resound in the present-day etheric body only through the powers of the creative resonance of an order higher than that of the astral forces of normal consciousness. This vital body normally operates in the process of human reproduction by escaping the "I," which is enveloped in pleasure and which wrongly, by means of pleasure, believes that it penetrates the Mystery while in reality, *it is always removed from it, so that it does not spoil it.* Right from the outset, this body of the light of life remained intact, uninvolved in the luciferic influences necessary to the cognitive human experience.

It is the original part of the etheric body, which remains in us as a vehicle of the creative powers of sound, and with which we can re-establish a relationship only if we bring consciousness to the fundamental correlation with its own powers of thinking, namely with a universal light of thinking, which is the emerging force of the Paraclete in the world.

Those of us who begin with sex cannot arrive at the spirit. We must begin with the spirit to arrive at sex. Love that truly begins to unite the couple is the force of the life currents that held souls together before they succumbed to sexual necessity. This is not about the human etheric body, but the astral body's relationship to the etheric-physical organism. To the degree that such a relationship unduly involves consciousness through thinking's dependence on the cerebral instrument, we are unable to perceive that the power of sex does not begin with sex, but with the astral forces illicitly colluding with the etheric-physical processes of sex and drawing, by means of the nervous system, the sensual lustful element from the collusion.

This sensual element, ascending as the ruler in the soul, gives rise to the various types of love—from the carnal to the sentient, to the passionate, to the compassionate, to the affective, to the attachment of blood-relationships or of family customs or of coexistence. At each level, it lives parasitically off the light drawn from its spiritual principle. *It is the sincere pretense of love,* the sentient story-line of love, whose outcome is inevitably disillusionment. Even through such forms of recitation, which can take a lifetime, the sacred element of love that operates secretly tends to heal by means of pain.

The proof of sacred love is the disenchantment of all levels of the "luciferic" form of love, right up to that which seems the most legitimate—compassion. Compassion is a faculty so elevated, that it would be difficult for it to pass through the paths of the *ego.* As egoic human beings, we should be compassionate, or charitable. We must consider, however, that we are looking at the esoteric meaning of the faculties in relation to sacred love. At a given moment of the experience, there is the evidence of the recognition of Lucifer's dominion within feeling. A legitimate attitude like compassion may prove to be deceptive if it interrupts a communion with the principle, from which alone the form of feeling can flow toward others. In other words, the source of sacred love, by not allowing human emotions or sentiments extraneous to its own wellspring, demands true compassion, which does not impede love.

If radicalness in that direction is to be achieved, we must realize that *each flow of human feeling is ruled by sex*. As long as it is bound to corporeality, human feeling cannot but be the expression of sex—even filial or maternal or paternal love. This is the theme, regarding which Freud had reasons to put forward as fact, a picture of the confusion of motives, the psychic states of fact, devoid of their inner background, which he was unable to glimpse. Thus, he made the problem essentially a dead-end and, yet, equipped with all the semblances of a formulation that corresponds to reality.

Love cannot come from the body, but from the spirit. Nevertheless, to realize it as that which comes from the spirit, is a long path riddled with deceptions and seductions, which are tests, whose meaning is ordinarily derived from life catastrophes, or from death. Only when he has the strength to free himself from the ties that maternal affection provides him can Parsifal move toward capturing the Grail. One must be worthy of having sentiments—such as compassion or charity— come from the spirit, and not be a betrayal toward the spirit, a temptation that disrupts sacred love. The series of noble feelings is necessary for human ethics, as a surrogate of the real dedication to the spirit. Even yesterday, such ethics could benefit from spiritual inspiration, mediated by priests and traditions. Such an inspiration has run out. By now, there cannot be any other that does not arise from the inner decision of those called upon to rediscover sacred love.

The couple's love must ultimately discover its uniqueness and its capacity to be exclusive, before it can express itself as love for one's neighbor and for the world. It is a simple ethical fact, or one of human relationship—undoubtedly positive, obvious in its naturalness—that, along the path, such a love as charity is exercised, to which one will not make the mistake of giving spiritual value in the sense of the mentioned change of consciousness. To pour out love toward others and the world is a possibility that is achieved if one has come to such a fullness of self that one can act beyond the individual limit. As long as that limit governs human action, the most charitable act is a *mâyâ*—even if ethically necessary—that responds to a given *dharma*. The present world provides us a panorama of a series of people and of currents at war with each other, each trying to overpower the other for the sake of a good that it presumes to bring to the other.

The *mâyâ* of feeling, which is the soul's subtle subjugation to sex, is surpassed only by the path along which Parsifal rediscovers access to the Grail, namely the path of the *sacred return,* which applies fidelity to the oneness of love, within whose core lies the germ of feeling's universal radiance. Only faithful love can pour itself out toward others, without betraying the identity with the being that is loved. Fidelity is the form of a transcendent accord, whose adamantine nature cannot be contaminated by subsequent relations of human feeling. But prior to this adamantine level, feeling demands to be guided by the discipline of a devotion, whose *intransigence can be controlled each hour of the day.*

According to the teaching of the Master of the new times,[*] what we have truly lost is not the Logos, but Isis-Sophia, *the inner woman, namely the ineffable secret of devotion.* Lucifer has kidnapped Isis. Therefore, we must penetrate the kingdom of Lucifer, if we want to rediscover the bearer of Divine Love. Every form of love, or affection, or *bhakti,* can be the deception of Lucifer. We truly have not lost the Logos, because self-consciousness is the form of the Logos obscurely emerging, the virile polarity of the androgynous element, which remains the sterile capacity of self-affirmation if it is not enlivened by the principle of primordial sonority, or of the *music of the spheres,* whose symbol is the Virgin crowned with stars—Isis-Sophia. We truly have lost the inner woman, or the sacredness of devotion, the fire of sacred love, the real *kundalini.*

The recovery of Isis-Sophia is therefore our decisive struggle against Lucifer. Lucifer, overcome in the heavens by Michael and on Earth by Christ, must be overcome in the human soul. *We humans have never defeated Lucifer.* Regarding such a task, Wolfram von Eschenbach warns that whosoever wants to access

---

[*]   Rudolf Steiner

the power of the Grail must open up the path with weapons in hand. The undertaking is essentially to recapture the precious jewel, once lost by Lucifer, then lost by humanity through the work of Lucifer. It was returned to the hands of the Lord at the Last Supper, and then brought back to human beings by the Guardians of the Grail. Parsifal's undertaking is essentially his continuous struggle against the hidden danger of Lucifer until the moment when, one Good Friday, Trevrezent communicates to him the Mystery of Death and of the Resurrection—namely, the content of the Sacred Cup.

The deception of Lucifer consists in love's dependence on the vastness of the reign of reflected light, where even the most elevated or mystical form of feeling depends profoundly on the body, or on sex. This can give the measure of heroics of the undertaking, which tends to free the angelic being, or the celestial woman within our inner depths. By such a path, the soul realizes within itself the gift of the Redeemer. Lucifer ceases to be an inner divinity that controls us through mystical, religious, or amorous feeling.

The "I" can free Isis-Sophia from the dominion of Lucifer if it manages to go beyond the astral body governed by Lucifer, who rules there to the extent that he established his reign there even before the "I" connected with the astral to take on corporeality. Through this dominion, the "I" identifies with the astral and the astral with the body. We humans act in accordance with the current of Lucifer, believing that we are free. Expressed within each feeling we have is not us, but the impulse of Lucifer.

The "I" recovers its own pure being if it transcends the astral—the sphere where Amfortas loses his battle. The "I" can recover the direct relationship with the *original vital body,* whose sonorous-luminous lymph operates intact in sex, outside the voluptuous contamination, which regards the astral and the area of the etheric body enslaved to it.

The "I's" relationship to the "life body" is a possibility that must not be contemplated in function of sexual magic—which at this point makes no sense, or ceases to have the meaning attributed to it by certain human schemes—but as a measure of value of sacred love, of the element of absolute purity or of independence from desire. Lucifer as the instigator of *eros* ceases to be an inner divinity of ours, to the extent that the "I"-Logos within the soul reconnects itself to the original celestial entity, the Virgin-Sophia. This is the meaning of reducing the "I's" relationship with corporeality to a pure duality, thanks to the elimination of the astral. In reality, it is not the astral that is eliminated but, rather, Lucifer. Once Lucifer is removed, the freed astral body is the soul restored to the original light, the Virgin-Sophia, the celestial bride, the light that shines intact on the waters, *Stella Maris*.

One can understand how the spiritual practice of pure perception, or of perceiving the light of entities, is essentially a discipline of silence of the Luciferic astral or of the purification of the astral. The "I" is brought directly to meet perception. Even here, a clear sensory duality is set up, "I"-world, or "I"-body, which reveals the possibility of a total synthesis of the "I"—already afoot in the unconscious simplicity of perception. Therefore, its *animadversio* (observation) is the principle of the unalterable calm, namely what in chapter V is called *Christic ataraxia*—over which earthly malice no longer has power, given that it can hurt humans only by making use of Lucifer's bite, of the Obstructer that lives off of human affections, such as hatreds, passions, exaltations and the depressions of the soul.

Lucifer's bite is taken away; the relationship exists between the "I" and the world, or between the "I" and being. But this relationship is the mystery of the soul rediscovered: if being is, the "I" is the original being. Being is the correlation with the other partner's soul. Each higher faculty can now awaken, to the extent that it is a power incarnated as life in the other. Through the androgynous complementarity, each person finds as a *power* within the soul what is *acting* in the living being of the other. The measure of the correlation is the presence of the unambiguous adamantine element, which has united the couple from the very beginning, and which can manifest its connection only in the form of superhuman love—namely, the love that always emerges and disperses in human love. The sacred binomial is reconstituted, when it becomes aware of its intangibility, which has remained unaltered in time, as it was before time.

8.

FIDELITY AS A SACRED CHOICE

A principle that can be derived from what we have thus far considered, is that the love of the human couple on earth has its foundation in a superhuman reality. Another truth not deducible from the preceding, and yet correlative to it, is that our spiritual undertaking, there, where it is a prelude to Initiation—on the brink of overcoming the individual and human limit—demands, as a decisive form, the experience of sacred love. One must see what relationship such supra-sensory presuppositions have to the human element.

A supernatural principle lies at the foundation of human love, giving signs of itself in the culminating moments of the couple's romantic accord; but it is unrecognized by them, and gradually separates itself as the life of feeling. It resounds according to a music whose transcendence is hardly repeatable. Each of the two would like to hear it again, but this music cannot be reintroduced because it becomes unknowingly rejected by the illusory thirst of life of one of the two (partners), or of both, and therefore, it returns to conceal itself in the "upper darkness" of the soul, where it continues to act indirectly, as a power of destiny. When it awakens, human love has a tragic course, if it is not illuminated by the light of knowledge. If its transcendence minimally bears its experience to the level of the conscious will, it can be recognized as the profound reality of the "I." The higher "I" is truly the source of the cosmic current of love.

Sacredness cannot but be the ultimate aim of the love between the couple, the coronation of a process that draws its content from a world that transcends the human, even though consciousness bases itself on the forgetfulness of such a world. Therefore, each real love in relation to the presupposed content is tragic. The two (partners) tend to coagulate in the human appearance the impulse that urges from the non-human sphere, but they each lack the adequate means to recognize it. The impulse comes in more than one moment to reveal its strength, which knows no limit. The two believe they take it on and realize it, without noticing that they essentially prepare what will eliminate the forms where they tend to realize it, because they identify the force with that of it which is grasped by corporeal nature—longing. Love, as inner tension, is longing even when the couple believes it to be incorporeal or spiritual, and even if the incorporeal in certain exceptional moments succeeds in resounding like supernatural music.

The incorporeal of the love impulse is what should incarnate, but it cannot, because its power is alienated in becoming an everyday ordinary sentiment. The situation of those who feel within themselves the super-human power of the impulse becomes contradictory, to the extent that they are led to realize it in forms that destroy it, not because it is unable to manifest in those forms, but because to this end it needs the vehicle of the soul that is intact. It can flow into the human being as long as it is not altered.

The soul does not gather the force according to the metaphysical impulse that such a force bears, but as a potential of its own tension toward the forms in which it believes it actualizes this impulse. The *sacred*, unknown but elusive, deteriorates into the *'enchanting'*; it dies away into the current of reflected light, into the processes of longing. Love's original will becomes desire. Desire cannot but shatter into the total non-correspondence of forms in which it tends to be satisfied. Thus, it is attracted to ever new objects of the deprivation of which it is a manifestation.

In the moment the soul is enamored, however, the urging of the original force gives rise to a state of blessedness. The soul is rekindled with the unconscious hope of rediscovering, in communion with the other, its original kingdom. But the soul makes a wrong move; it is once again subjected to the deception of Lucifer. It goes to meet the apparent being of the other, but not that of the other being which demands it and awaits it. The moment of falling in love is a transcendent experience that tends to re-establish itself, but it can give itself only to the awakened forces of consciousness. The two (partners) feel unusually independent of the human limit. They feel they are near a realm that is penetrable thanks to an evocable magical force. But they disregard the evocative formula; they ignore the itinerary of the Grail.

In that moment, to speak of eternal love, of the uniqueness of self-giving, of absolute fidelity, is true. That is when the couple unknowingly touches the *sublime*: the mystery from which their encounter arises. For a while, despite being within the "Serpent's" circuitous force, they gather within themselves another type of force, namely that of the primordial impulse that has always defeated the Serpent. If they were to find, within themselves, the principle of the distinction, they would know that love does not arise from the body, nor even from the soul but, rather, from the spirit. They would seek the spirit through love, which is love's real task. They would seek the spirit as an inexhaustible source of love. They would then know the mystery of the soul.

It is evident that what is needed is an act of consciousness capable of connecting with the event's supernatural element, which the couple—as an initiatic couple—can tap into only by means of a magical path. But one does not pass from one level of such an experience to another by way of a simple intuition and the correlative decision. In fact, it is has nothing to do with a passage, but with transcendence. The undertaking of sacred love, beyond the inner development of the couple and the apprenticeship of the reciprocal devotion—which continuously overcomes the impediment inherent in human nature—requires the attainment of an adamantine element, the sense and support of the whole work: *fidelity*, as reciprocal fidelity and (fidelity) to the Spirit, which is *the same fidelity*.

Due to the absence of such an element, enduring love is not possible on earth; true love is not possible. Fidelity is usually considered a limit that is placed on oneself, through devotion or respect toward the other. We are unable to conceive it as the mode of being of an unlimited principle, which, with all autonomy, can assume life, so that it does not have to contradict any servitude to desire, namely to the desire that we ordinary beings mistake for inner necessity, legitimate need, the right of life.

Even when fidelity, more than an ethical value, is an offer of the soul to the beloved, it almost always springs from self-sacrifice, or from a positive opposition to longing that automatically receives more and more subsequent solicitations from the multiplicity of outer stimuli. It is not the result of an inner necessity, of a capacity to forget itself and to give according to a fullness of soul, which is beyond all bonds or all needs. Those who encounter the other's soul within the circuit of the spiritual absolute find (within this soul) what can arise from a synthesis of all earthly experiences. Fidelity is, therefore, the form of total self-giving to the spirit, the inner process, the *continuity.*

Outer fidelity usually has inner infidelity as its price, to the extent that longing can be contradicted, contrasted, on behalf of a given word or of a sacrament to which one feels bound, but not excluded. Genuine fidelity is, instead, the impossibility for longing to continue manipulating the soul, when this soul encounters the other soul outside the Serpent's circuit, in the sidereal circuit that governs each coil of the Serpent.

Therefore, it has to do with a level higher than that of human fidelity. It is the discovery of the spiritual unity within oneself and, therefore, with the other, which concludes the cycle of decadence of the soul, incessantly attracted by one form to another, according to a thirst for life that cannot be extinguished in any fulfillment. The resolution of fidelity is to overcome the need to depend on the ancient deception, because such a need does not regard the living soul but its dead aspect that has become the consciousness by means of which the ego is able to live. Deception is discovered through disillusionment, that is, in its confrontation with pain or with death. *Sacred love is, in fact, the force that overcomes pain and death.*

Fidelity is the fundamental technique of the Spirit. It is the final teaching that Parsifal receives from Trevrezent on Good Friday, before recovering the Grail. The whole point of fidelity is for the "I" to rediscover its own pure essence, as a flow of the supra-sensory toward the sensory within the current of longing. Out of love for the other, such a current can be retraced, given that the true experience of the senses is not sensory, but supra-sensory. Since longing is the inclination toward the senses, the lustful soul does not achieve the true experience of the senses. The content of the senses that is longed for escapes it. This 'being taken' by the senses, uses the forces of love for a *congressus** that destroys the very life of love, the Tree of Life. In order for the Grail to be restored, the soul's relation must be recognized as the spirit's remote task—a prenatal decision of the "I." The beloved cannot be longed for but, rather, desired free within its "I," so that it can express its real inner dimension. Fidelity is not what is ordinarily meant by it, but what it conceals—the pure potential of freedom.

Fidelity is hard to comprehend because it is a sacred choice, which restores the original moment of the couple's accord based on Divine Willing. Therefore, it is a level beyond words. No human quality, unless understood as a mystical movement aroused by the supernatural, corresponds to its name—namely, fidelity to the Divine outside of the human, not to the Divine that appears within the human. It is instead the loyalty toward the truth of ourselves, the veneration of the reality that allows itself to be recognized and contemplated in a living being, which, for man is the woman that sums up the whole universe. Therefore, it is the beginning of love toward the whole universe. In order for it to become human reality, it must actualize within itself its own universal element. It must be universal love. The other half of the couple, as the re-awakener, reawakened, bears the universe within itself.

With regard to the transcendence of the original motion, fidelity can be understood as the impulse that hides something that its word only says symbolically, almost suggestive of a quality which once lived by its own *dynamis,* no longer retrievable today. Therefore, fidelity is thought of as a virtue that requires self-limitation, while in reality it is the expression of the limitlessness of the principle according to which the restorative accord begins.

This is the unspeakable virtue of the relationship, whereby man finds in woman a substantial and mysterious element, which, solicited, erupts as a power of obscuration or of resurrection,

---

*　　companionship/sexual intercourse

depending on the purity, or on the fidelity with which he reaches out to her. Purification in this sense is fidelity, which operates up to the place responsive to the degradation of the human being— the one that brought about *cosmic infidelity*.

The course of this restorative will of the movement as it was in the beginning, actualizes the transcendent intent from which it sprang. Its absence, infidelity, is death. Its presence is *the sacred choice,* the resurrection. According to a remote teaching, Initiates find outside themselves, in the world and in things, the purity that they have within them. Everything that is impure starts from them; it is not in the world. Thus, the newfound fidelity is the impossibility that the other grows dim, or decays, or is arrested. One's fidelity, or sacred choice, is the resurgent life of the other.

That Good Friday, Parsifal understood his own sacred choice, namely the meaning of his fidelity to Kondwiramur, as fidelity to the Grail. Although he was still unfamiliar with the Mystery of Christ, he remained connected to it by being faithful to his lady. When he had brought down the invincible Gramoflanz, this same Gramoflanz wanted to know who his conqueror was. Upon hearing Parsifal utter his own name, Gramoflanz said, "I am happy because I die at the hands of a best knight in the world." Orgeleuse had come to offer herself as a reward to the victor, but Parsifal rejected her, saying to her: "I did not fight for you," and he resumed his journey.

9.

TRANSCENDENCE, NOT SUBLIMATION

A lucid experience of the relationship allows us to glimpse within it the circuit of a force, whose reality turns out to be extraneous to *eros*. It is possible to see this force spring from a polarity opposite to that of sex, from a supernatural realm. Incarnating and degrading, it manifests within us as an emotional sentiment and, more deeply, as erotic sexuality, altered and obtuse. Normally we manage to be conscious of such a force, not because we feel it, but because we make use of it to feel ourselves. Therefore, we have the impression that it arises from the body, or from the psychosomatic being. We believe that the force that manifests in sex belongs to the generative organs.

In reality, it is a current of life, of a supra-sensory nature, that barely manifests in the phenomenology of sex, since we cannot sustain its objective power and vastness. Its source can only be the perception of moments of the higher "I," which cannot be fixed by ordinary memory. Its appearance as a weaving of human history does not occur so that we can make it subservient to ourselves and degrade it but, rather, so that we can again, by means of it, rise up to our true nature. This task is revealed to the couple when the souls' encounter occurs according to an absolute will, which does not allow itself to be led astray by earthly deception. As a kindling of love, the supernal life flows simultaneously into the couple's soul, but in this lies the couple's obligation toward the world, the awareness of a secret of salvation that must be transmitted.

They can be worthy of understanding that the transcendent content of such a supernal life becomes an *individual* experience only to the degree in which it has their *extra-individual* relationship as a vehicle. Souls can give rise to a lost, original correlation. An adamantine element of this (correlation), which operates autonomously and inescapably, is reawakened. The objective encounter of the fluidic currents, vehicles of extra-temporal impulses, renders the accord fateful. The reciprocal integration of the fluidic currents is made possible by ensuring them their incorporeal movement. Thanks to non-corporeality, the force flows according to its real nature, coming to life again, identical, in the soul of each (partner), as the light of "paracletic" life. The adamantine element, therefore, acts as an archetype of a transmission of the Grail's ultimate content to human individuality.

Within the archetypal entity, the androgynous character can be recognized, reforming itself thanks to a mutual exchange of the soul's currents, according to a movement not conditioned by corporeality but, rather, only by an etheric vehicle that corresponds to it. The feeling of sacred love frees the etheric body from the physical support, for what is necessary to its harmony with the soul's currents of light, that is, with its potential androgynous state. The sex of the etheric body, in fact, is diametrically opposite to that of the physical body, while the astral body is constitutionally androgynous in itself.

By virtue of this etheric harmony, the archetypal entity reacquires an identical power of light and of life, which is the resurgent virtue of the *dyadic one,* or of the Androgyny, within the soul of each one. Illuminated is its sense of sacred love, namely the possibility for its dynamic form to experience the rediscovered harmony, insofar as each of the two (partners) ritually operates from the underlying unity, that is, from the soul's original structure. The couple does not have to create anything new. The couple must only consciously reawaken what has existed from the very beginning, hidden at a transcendent level of consciousness, to which (in states of wakefulness) only the virtue of the accord can elevate—the binary masculine-feminine element of one soul corresponding to the binary feminine-masculine element of the other. The restoration of the binomial-quadrinomial accord renders the soul independent of the corporeal categories that it needs for earthly experience; but, for this reason, it confers to it a power of orientation of this experience.

The concept of the absolute estrangement of the original power of *eros* to the sexual sphere can help us understand how spiritual love is not a sublimation of a physical phenomenology. Each form of sexual sublimation is undeniably positive, but from the viewpoint of the genuine experience, it remains closed within the limits of corporeality. Regardless of the heights that can be reached by this form of sublimation, *the sublimation of longing does not escape the sphere of desire.* A sublimated dependence does not cease to be dependence, which is always a dependence on the Serpent's power.

Sacred love is not the spiritualization of sensual love but, rather, the opposite. It presents itself as a metaphysical surge that strikes the human being—taking on or resolving sex. Having nothing in common with sex as it results to human sensuality, it manages to establish its own relationship with sex. Sacred love, alone, can achieve communion with the original forces of life and of sound, which, remaining unknown to consciousness, operate within the human being by penetrating the reproductive process. *They are forces with which only the sanctity of the soul can have a relationship—the sanctity of the soul* where the Principle (the incorporeal absolute) that sustains corporeality from the depths is present.

The powers of sound, or of the Word, operate within the sexual experience and within the generative process, dominating, through the objectivity of these, the fluidic element of the Serpent, which keeps the soul bound to it by means of desire. Such powers can ascend within the soul thanks to an autonomous radical movement of the "I," with respect to desire. They can manifest as forces of sacred love, capable of restoring the primordial music of the correlation between man and woman. They bear within the individual soul the power of the "music of the spheres" as a cosmic force of the earthly correlation, giving to each one a genuine sense of life, because it is the most harmonious and heroic of all creative virtues. Its purpose is to rediscover the original accord, so that *the human couple can be reconstituted as the celestial couple.* From its capacity of generation, a human type whose nature does not constitute an opposition to the Spirit can arise.

Even though consciousness does not surface minimally

from it, *this love is awaited by the Earth*; it is awaited by us as the highest hope—of a human regenerative lifeblood of the human being. In truth, the human encroaches into the subhuman. The animal element awakens in people. Humanity awaits the introduction of a heroic force, because it is regenerating. Yet, we do not know from where it can arise. We fail to imagine the source from which it can spring. The human mental, the dialectical mental that expresses the Serpent's reign, cannot conceive the emergence of a love whose force does not depend on the corporeal realm, which is to say, on the Serpent's influence.

For this reason, the undertaking of sacred love is initiatic. But, at its solitary and sublime level, it constitutes the model for all human love that nevertheless (even though occurring in the kingdom of the Obstructers) always tends obscurely to rediscover the ancient light of life, according to the soul's original forces. There is no love that, flashing between man and woman on earth, does not unknowingly tend to operate as sacred love. There is a moment in each encounter between man and woman—that is not a mechanical exchange of corporeal sensations—where love flows as an incorporeal force. That moment can be saved and directed if sacred love begins to blossom on Earth by virtue of rare beings capable of the initial movement of self-giving. Their force is the simultaneous recognition of the task, namely the mutual consecration for the communion of the light of consciousness with the creative powers of life and sound, present in the sphere of willing and operating metaphysically in sex.

It is helpful to look with clarity at the uselessness or the extreme harm of current methods of magic and sex, which presume to go to the root of the problem. They attract naïve or lazy investigators who wish to avoid the effort of knowing themselves and their own defects as limits to be overcome for an effective supra-sensory experience. By means of such methods, they attempt a sort of integration into the dynamic current of sex, thanks to a technique that artificially tends to solicit it and to control it. The error of those who follow such methods is to believe they have something to do with the force and not with more acute corporeal sensations. By means of sex, or the ingestion of specific substances, one experiences one's own fluidic zone energized beyond normal consciousness. Behind sufficient excitation, the fluidic dynamisms are led to an extra-normal mobility, which consciousness should assume and utilize in a yogic way.

The naivety of such highly skilled means consists in presupposing a principle of power, whose confirmation it seeks in a potential for desire, which is its deprivation. Two concepts are at the core of such a naïve position—the concept of sublimation and that of willfully capturing the force. Both are sufficiently plausible, in relation to the lack of knowledge of the work's original substance and to the principle to which one must appeal. It is inevitable to move from the conditions of desire, but it is equally inevitable to remain bound to it, because of a technique that, ignoring the constitutional need of desire, ends up reinforcing it. Klingsor essentially became the adversary of the Grail, to the extent that he was a victim of the desire for power. The purpose of his emasculation was the abstract chastity of the body, that is, the illusion of realizing the spirit by means of a corporeal fact or an act of desire.

No sublimation of sex can allow us to control its metaphysical force. *A radical way is needed*—a heroic way. We must understand what within our inner life reveals a principle of independence from the instinctive sphere as an immediate absolute. Only a force of equal and deeper intensity can be juxtaposed to the profound drive of desire (which is the only force capable of connecting human consciousness with *eros* and with the erotic-generative act)—namely a force that can connect the higher virtue of consciousness to the generative sphere, as was the case in the beginning for the superhuman couple, to which was possible a *celestial consciousness alongside generative needs,* given that the union of bodies occurred in a state of impersonal transcendence, as if in a dream state.

Only a force that knows its source outside of that desire which nonetheless confines the soul within the sentient-corporeal limit can be juxtaposed. Abstract thought, pure logical thought, is the only activity that, although rising from the soul's original movement of desire, is alienated from the soul, becoming reflected, devoid of life—devoid of desire, mathematical or logical. This thinking is cut off from the soul. But, for this reason, it is *the "I"'s chance to operate outside of the soul, or outside of the sphere of desire*. Normally, there is no relationship between this abstract thought and the "I." This thinking, in fact, oblivious of its own power, proceeds according to automatism, constructing for its use and consumption its own "I," its psyche, its scientific systems, its culture. The real "I" is unknown to it.

But the "I" can establish, volitionally, a relationship with this lifeless thought. It then rises up as the soul's element of life. In reality, the ultimate aim of such thought is to die to the point of a possible resurrection. It is a matter of willing it to the point of exhaustion, so that along the same lines there appears the will that willed it, a new will, devoid of presuppositions, free of psychic ties, unconditioned. By means of this dead thinking, the "I" can be willed according to a pure movement that restores the breath of life and light to the soul. Thinking and willing find a deeper harmony—feeling. There is a discipline of concentration and of meditation, proper to today's human being, indistinguishable from the resurrection of feeling, that corresponds to the soul's original structure. From here, a power of incorporeal love can be kindled, capable of acting beyond corporeality—as reflected thought or ordinary mental picturing abstractly can—*with the impetus of immateriality of a pure idea and, nevertheless, with the intensity of a powerful passion.* Something like platonic love that has become a non-consuming flame, a flame of total awareness, a devotion of total will, at the bottom of a musical sidereity, or of a devotion that is gratitude towards the spirit revealed by the figure of light of the other (partner). The musicality of this platonic love is recognized as a presence, within the soul, of the forces of the Word—or of the original life and sound—capable of defeating the Serpent.

The original music enchants the Serpent—the natural enchanter of the soul. The virtue of physical generation rises again as the virtue of an inner generation, which draws its highest creative power from the physical depths. Overcoming the limit is the moment of an intense human crisis, in which the evidence of each lower constraint occurs. One finds oneself before a supernatural current of life, aimed at breaking the enchantment of the soul's apparent death. It strikes consciousness with the violence of a force that annihilates life to awaken it at another level.

The self-donation of sacred love is not a mystical fact, or a form of *bhakti,* but a *higher act of will*—a heroic determination. The presupposition is self-transcendence, attainable by a meditative path, or the noesis of pure thinking. We have spoken about *Christic ataraxia,* as well as the underlying mood of the soul that prepares for such an experience, namely the stripping of every vanity, the readiness for the radical test of autonomy with respect to the bonds of desire. In reality, it is primarily about overcoming an internal limit of thinking. Such an overcoming leads to a communion with the impersonal powers, or Spiritual Hierarchies, that support personal feeling and willing. The light of thinking reconnecting with the powers of warmth and of life is the process of sacred love.

The experience provides the lucid realization that *the forces of love have nothing to do with sex,* even though they bind themselves to sex by way of a sentient alteration of their original nature. Therefore, each form of sublimation is a spiritual form of renouncing the reintegration; it is to believe that it is about elevating a lower force. Meanwhile, the task consists in realizing, below, a supernal force that already acts within the soul, but unknown: a force that does not undergo a transformation, but demands to transform. This supernal force calls for the advent of real self-consciousness, or the sacrifice of illusory consciousness—the perception of reality beyond *mâyâ,* that is, beyond the veil of Isis-Hecate.

Supra-sensory perception allows for encountering, in the other (partner), a golden-adamantine being, which is his or her true being, namely the "I" in its vestment of light, visible as far as the fluidic corporeal form—the true and eternal being of the other. But this super-mental being, which is seen as if it were liberated above the head of the other, is one with the "I" of the one who contemplates it in its vestment of light. We realize this "I" insofar as we see it as one with the metaphysical being of the other. It is impossible to experience the "I" if we do not manage to see the golden-adamantine being of the other, which is his or her reality, with which we continuously need to make contact, so that human appearance cannot divert the task of sacred love.

There is a sort of sidereal altar where one can contemplate the figure of the other in its grandeur and in its eternity, with the light's infinite richness of differentiations or hierarchies. That figure, once seen, becomes the symbol that can continuously be evoked by means of the higher feeling that it alone has been able to evoke.

10.

The Sense of "Platonic Love"

We could perceive the forces of sex, namely the deepest forces operating within the human being, if we raise our waking consciousness to the level in which deep sleep occurs. At such a condition, these forces would cease to be destructive. They, in fact, carry out their creative work right down to the sensory (realm), within a sphere that contradicts their supra-sensory nature.

To perceive the process of sex only sensually and not to be conscious of the perceptive content is the contradiction in which *sin* can be said to consist: into which we otherwise incur continually, inasmuch as we continually perceive the living but without having it as a *sensation*. In fact, the living is for us a representation, not a sensorial experience, despite its presence in perception.

We have seen how the original couple was "immune from sin," insofar as their sexual act took place independently of consciousness, to which sexual intercourse was essential and carried out exclusively as a beatific union of souls. Longing and sin were born from perception and, therefore, from the correlative knowledge of a process whose objective content the soul was unable to gather. They were born out of *sensation*, which began to resound within the soul as an egoic reaction that engages the highest forces, unperceived, within the sensory (realm).

And we have mentioned how this gathering of sensation that is devoid of its inner content, and that conditions only as a physical value, was the way for consciousness to arrive at self-consciousness, in line with limiting itself to physical finiteness. The inner connection of sex was lost to the benefit of an awareness of the sensory, namely of individual consciousness.

We can grasp the sense of what will be the task of the restoration, or of the Resurrection, symbolized by the redemption of the Grail, if we bear in mind that the birth of self-consciousness was due to the binding of the soul to the physical brain. In fact, during the Edenic period, the original couple could effectively keep the reciprocal communion of light intact, since the spiritual instrument of self-consciousness—the brain—was not ready. The brain would have put each of the two in a position to elaborate, by means of their own inner activity, the world's content, tending to appear to us exclusively as sensory. *Appearance would gradually become reality.* That the semblance could be illegitimately identified with reality, since the human being's inner activity must be subjected to the conditions of cerebral mediation, was initially and, for a considerable time, inevitable.

Since, for the soul, the brain is the mediator of the spirit regarding earthly experience, such experience is inevitably the experience of appearance, or of *mâyâ,* given that it is exclusively sensory. Therefore, the spirit's relationship with the sensory (realm), through perception, would become longing. The spirit, mediated by cerebralism, leaves within itself a spiritual world, toward which it blindly tends. The sensory (realm) is offered to it as immediate; a sensory (realm) behind which lies the world it is losing and with which it frantically seeks to keep the communion intact, in a traditional and ritualistic sense. But unlike before, such a communion is no longer possible. *The immediate reality is no longer the supra-sensory,* but the sensory, toward which human beings turn ever more, with *all* their inner power, willing it as they might will *the absolute*, which to them begins to be internal and extra-conscious. This force of willing, aimed at an object unrelated to its spiritual level, is *longing.*

Therefore, in the sexual sphere, the highest powers, operating according to an untouchable pattern of sanctity, assume the sacrifice of reproduction diverted toward the animal form, necessary for the new human condition—the sensory realm's subjection to longing. We participate in the reproductive act only through sensation, in which the etheric element—necessary for eliminating any intervention of consciousness—is inserted.

Thus, we die to our spiritual nature. Longing, as the spirit's striving toward the sensory form estranged from its supra-sensory foundation, makes it assume, as its own nature, a corporeality from which *the connection with the perpetuity of life is removed*; for this reason, death is inevitable—until the day we can discover the connection, by means of the new forces of consciousness.

There is no spiritual practice, or inner resurrection, that for us does not involve the real knowledge of our relationship to sex. Such knowledge, by actualizing its own radical nature, demands that the conscious principle rediscover the mystery of generation outside the bondage to desire. Likewise, it can be said that there is no inner reintegration, or Initiation, that does not undergo the resolution of desire and the restoration of the soul's relationship with the pure *forces of warmth and of life* operating in sex. Such is the purpose of Parsifal's undertaking, which fails at first, because his "I" still lacks the sufficient forces of independence with respect to his lower nature. He can bring about the recovery of the Grail when he is able to reacquire the power of the Sacred Spear, or the *solar power* with respect to his *lunar nature.*

Whoever is familiar with the path of pure perception understands how the contemplative spiritual practice of the sensory (realm)—in particular of the mineral and of the plant—constitutes the precondition to such a reintegration, since it leads to the perception of the original forces of feeling and willing, which connect the sense organs to the center of the heart. Without such a connection, sensorial perception would be impossible. This is the result of *an agreement of supra-sensory forces* with sensory processes, given to the human being but which, as such, is *unknown* to us. Such a gift is a transcendence that we use daily, by means of the senses, without sensing its value.

The agreement must be truly recognized, so that what is required of the soul to ensure a perception of *eros* can be understood. The operation, which is simple in front of a crystal or a flower, is nonetheless the model of its actualization in the encounter with the most arduous and dynamic content of erotic sensation. The difficulty before which everyone comes to a halt is the fear of an absolute 'wanting to be' in this redemption, which, demanding a new dimension of feeling, presents itself as a task that cannot be evoked by ordinary memory. Even here, the meaning of a "drink of memory," can help us understand the moment when Parsifal intuits the decisive task necessary for the re-consecration of the Grail; his intuiting is a remembering.

The most serious obstacle is the normal oblivion of what is intuited in moments of self-transcendence. One must cultivate a feeling of devotion, which is the power of remembering the work's purpose, the image of its unspeakable content. The modern-day intellect lacks sufficient forces to grasp the movement of self-transcendence, even if at times it is capable of conceiving it dialectically.

Such transcendence is required to lift that which has been degraded and that mistakes the degree of the "fall" for its own grade, to *correct the wrong*, to restore what was removed, or lost. It is the undertaking of sacred love. One can understand how, (having) let go of the support of longing, the relationship of consciousness with the forces of the super-nature operating in sex, can only be supported through the vitalization of the soul's adamantine element, the deepest and most hidden, which realizes its original content—its super-nature. This content does not need the vehicle of desire to rise up as the power of life.

It is not a matter of mystical vitalization, but of the intense erupting of a will not solicited by anything other than its own force and, yet, capable of losing itself in the total giving of oneself to the other, according to an unlimited, terse luminous love which is in line with "platonic love," or with the devotion of the *gopî* of Krishna, or with the idealism of the "Fedeli d'Amore" of Il Dolce Stil Novo, but to arrive there, where no one has ever arrived, since it is not simply love for the Divine, or the annihilation of oneself in devotion, but love for a *(living) being,* where alone the Divine can be met in its intact mystery—a being whose temporal history is present with its non-temporal history, a synthesis of the history of the human being and the cosmos, a symbol of the path so far traveled for the recovery of the original accord. The reciprocity of the original accord's rediscovery is this love. It is a definitive event, which concludes a long cycle of consumption and of obscurity. In Wolfram von Eschenbach, Parsifal warns Gawain: "When you encounter the moment of battle, you will be aided by the thought of a woman."

Given the deep conditioning of ordinary consciousness with respect to the experience of sex, one can say that *platonic love* is the unconditioned correlation, since it is realized inevitably not by the affective (sentient) soul, but by the consciousness soul, that is, by that area of the soul which manifests *the initial independence of the "I" from corporeality.* It is love drawn from its own metaphysical source and that, therefore, receives within itself the force that dominates the physical, which lights up with an intensity capable of reaching into the corporeal depths, where previously only longing and lust reached. From this rediscovered union, it can equally attain a spiritual or physical birth.

The level of feeling, which feeds on its own supra-sensory source, is the same in which the soul experiences *pure thinking*, living ideas, or the celestial archetypes of things. The level is continuously attained by a communion of the couple, capable of overcoming the bodies' separation, when contingent necessities involve a temporary separation. The trial alluded to in the myth of Orpheus and Eurydice is metaphysically foreseen and has its temporary drama on the sensory plane. The separation, in its spatial-temporal contingency, is *the test for a more intense union of souls* beyond corporeal vehicles and for a refinement of the inner organs necessary for a communion of depth—a communion that must consciously restore the *adamantine synthesis.*

In the feeling that conjoins the couple, operates the presentiment of life that united the celestial couple, according to a transcendent and etheric harmony, which realized in the one the complement of the other. It is a complementarity connected to a superhuman presupposition, *i.e.,* to the fundamental androgynous order, for which each one bore within him or herself—as a *potential* element—that which integrated the corresponding *existing* element in the other. The original couple constituted the precondition for a divine birth in the human being.

In the epoch of the "I," or of the initial self-consciousness, the original couple is a point of departure, which can be rediscovered, given that its principle of synthesis corresponds to the nature of the "I." The "I" is the bearer of the reunification. The whole symbolism of the Grail alludes to the fact that such a point of departure can be rediscovered, as if it had never been lost. Joseph of Arimathea's agreement with the Angels and with the original Knights elected by the Lord regards the transmission of a *heroic task*, the recovery of a primordial good, left suspended outside of time, to be one day inserted into time, when human beings are ready, based on the initial experience of self over time, (based on) the clear experience of the "I." The *Guardians of the Sacred Cup* bear such a possibility inherent in the "I." Human love, when it manifests a super-individual impulse, is the obscure search for the Grail, or even of the restoration of a primordial condition, which demands living with the force of its non-temporality in time. The love of the couple must find its movement in itself, beyond the forms of semblance, so as to insert, within the experience of time, the impetus of its perpetuity.

As mentioned, the sense of "platonic love" is not to avoid the union of bodies and physical generation but, rather, to liberate the force of *eros* from desire, so as to restore the life of feeling and the warmth of willing to their true source, which is the heart. Platonic love is thus the level of sacred love, but this sacred love becomes the realization of that platonic love.

In the ordinary experience of *eros*, the sensation of lust is attributable to a profound traction of feeling that—grasped by the sensory process and removed from the mediation of the heart to which it should bear each of its resonances—is directly reflected in the nervous system and in the brain, which should instead receive the content of consciousness that communicates with the feeling of the heart. *Pleasure comes from feeling that is removed from the source of the heart* and that, therefore, has an illicit relationship with the instrument of consciousness—the nervous system—which compels consciousness to a content that such consciousness is unable to elaborate, since it is not autonomous with respect to it. In essence, with respect to sexual pleasure, consciousness is in a state of impotency and confusion. It is inevitably identified with a content about which it can say nothing, since this content imposes itself, by means of a feeling removed from its normal function and, therefore, incapable of a relationship according to the forces of which it is woven— namely, the forces of the heart.

Engaged in sensual pleasure, feeling—without which sensual

pleasure could not be felt as such, but would be a perception of another kind—does not belong to sex, but to the heart. The deviation of this feeling makes it possible for the content of the sexual act to impose itself directly on consciousness as a raw sensation, thereby remaining truly imperceptible to consciousness. It lacks the real vehicle— feeling—to the extent that such feeling is grasped and compelled to a resonance that alienates it from its reality, whose source is the heart. Normal perception, in fact, is objectively possible, thanks to an autonomous concurrence of the forces of willing, of feeling and of thinking in the perceptive act, according to *a movement perfect in its purity,* which, in the extra-conscious depths, unites them with their true source—the heart.

The illnesses of feeling and willing are all traceable to a breakdown of the relationship of the three faculties with the heart. Normal sensory perception, in the *perfection* of its dynamic scheme, as a process where the forces of the psychosomatic structure converge harmoniously, is a minimal balancing event of the whole life of the soul. It is, in a small way, *the model* of the objective function of feeling and willing with respect to the world's contents. It is important to bear in mind that the perfection of the inner process of perception is an extra-conscious reality, which consciousness must still acquire. This is the concrete starting point. The basis of the spiritual practice to which we have alluded as the present path to the Holy Grail is the discipline of *pure perception.*

In the sexual experience, the perceptive process is made chaotic by the prevalence of longing and of the lustful element, which is the exaltation of feeling with respect to a content whose relationship with the heart it does not manage to establish. Instead, in ordinary sense perception, the intervention of desire does not have the power to alter the regular function of feeling and of willing through the sensory organ. *Their relationship with the heart remains intact.* For the fact that light's element of life is not altered in ordinary perception, the objectivity of the content is possible. Such objectivity falls short in erotic perception. Feeling engaged in longing becomes sensual pleasure; it lacks the power to resonate with the sacred forces operating profoundly in sex, because the current of longing impedes it from connecting with the heart. The level of sensual pleasure is truly that of forgetting the real human level.

Outside the regularity of ordinary sensory perception, where feeling flows according to its original virtue, it is altered by its constraint to corporeality, that is, by having to resound according to thinking's constraint to cerebralism, which, as we have seen, is the origin of desire. In this way, feeling renounces being a vehicle of the heart, or of the human being's true force. It does not manage to be feeling with respect to the essential forces of willing called upon to operate in sex. Its alteration is the nourishment of lust.

The alteration of feeling becomes the alteration of the current of will by means of which consciousness is connected to sex. Nonetheless, the cosmic current of the will operates, simultaneously, according to the absoluteness of its autonomy and of its purity, in the reproductive process, even in the lower animal form. Such work is also required in infertile pairings and in the simple aim of pleasure. This is the sacrifice of the highest forces operating within the human being, for those of us subjected to the sensory sphere and to cerebral consciousness, devoid of the heart's source of life: so that we can one day encounter them by means of consciousness—which is to say, according to the path of sacred love.

From the source of the heart, feeling can draw the life needed for the relationship with the forces of willing that operate in sex and (that are) independent from it. But within the even greater transcendent depths of the heart, we can find the very source of such willing forces, of *albedo*[7], of *rubedo*[8], or the power of synthesis of the forces of the Sun and of the Moon, symbolized by the Cup of the Grail and the *Path of the Adamantine Knight*.

As we have seen, Lucifer can still operate within feeling, to the extent that we need reflected (or cerebral) thinking. The age of self-consciousness is the one which bears the possibility of passing from reflected thought to living thinking. This cannot mean that reflected thought should be abolished. It must become an instrument of real thinking, by no longer being subjected to illusory appearance and to the expressions of instincts. Thinking, in being able to elevate itself to *pure ideation,* has the key to reconnect feeling to the heart; which is to say, feeling reconnected with the heart has the key of sacred love, which is feeling that discovers within itself the power of life capable of re-establishing the purity of the soul's relationship with the forces operating in reproduction.

True beatitude belongs to this feeling connected to the heart, insofar as it is a *pure beatitude*, free of egoism and of passion, capable of a profound identity that, to be realized, does not need longing, because in such an identity, it has all that which is the object of its irradiating. It is the path to the discovery of Osiris, and his resurrection—namely, the virtue of the mighty love of Isis. The slain God would be resurrected, thanks to a cosmic power that would be brought to Earth by Christ. Yet, from that day on, Isis-Sophia would make it operative within human beings. *The path of sacred love is truly the undertaking of the Grail of the new times.*

The need for feeling re-enlivened according to platonic love, or according to the secret of heavenly Isis, or the content of the Grail Cup, is the relationship with the profound current of willing that operates metaphysically in sex. This relationship does not normally exist for human beings. The murky and even intense sensation of lust is born out of its breakdown. The resurrection of feeling restores the relationship with the profound force that operates in sex. This force does not belong to sex, but to our spiritual being, to that higher nature of ours which minimally and in a reflected way expresses itself as consciousness. Manifesting by means of sex, it seems to belong to sex, because the connection of reflected consciousness to sex produces the dependence of consciousness—by means of sensual pleasure—on its corrupt power, namely the power of the force that, in its integrity, is the foundation of consciousness.

The need to connect feeling with the heart, regarding the experience of *eros,* leads feeling to rediscover the divine element within itself and to restore to the current of will its connection to the heart. Such is the sense of platonic love, or of the soul's real relationship with the pure powers that intervene in the sexual act, without belonging to sex and without having any relationship with sensual pleasure. The pure kindling and the conscious exaltation of such love are our *true medicine,* because they invert (within us) the direction of the Fall. The relation with sex belongs solely to this love, according to an impulse totally founded in the spiritual and, therefore, capable of uniting with the sanctity of the forces that—unknown by ordinary human beings—make physical generation possible by sacrificing themselves.

The expression *'inversion of the fall'* regarding the current of feeling is equal to that of overcoming death, or of being resurrected from a state of obscurity similar to death. The experience of "platonic love," in fact, as a reconnection of the three faculties of the soul with the source of the heart, requires the trial of overcoming a darkness, which is the stratification in human nature of the levels of corruption of the ancient force. Only tapping into the wellspring of the force can provide a way to overcome the darkness.

The crucial test of human love is this: platonic love must pass through Golgotha if it wants to be realized as sacred love. The couple has to know the final spagyric operation of Gold or of Fire, which leads to the "Fountain in the secret of the Stone," or to the spiritual secret of physical corporeality, the ultimate content of the Grail: the couple must know the profound sacrifice of the soul's faculties, death and resurrection. Just as the three soul forces are present (according to an autonomous harmony) in sensory perception, they also tend to merge with the fullness of their power of life and of light within the current of human love, where ordinarily they are corrupted and lose their harmony, but they can flow united and express their secret of life and of light, where the consecration of souls keeps their superhuman nature intact to them in the human.

11.

The Initiatic Secret of the Serpent

From the cosmological references of the present study, the idea of the "music of the spheres"—as a remote vision of an invisible construct of the Universe, whose *dynamis* is the *creative sound*—appears decisive with regard to the treated theme. We have seen how the forces of the original sonority operate within us at a given moment, dominating in us the inferior lunar element, necessary for the reproduction of our vital-physical form.

Based on such a vision, our resurrection from the soul's apparent death can be justifiably conceived as the possibility for our awareness to open up to the vital current of the powers of sound, which are original to it. What has been called the soul's apparent death, as the effect of losing the vitalizing music, is its subjection to the power of the lunar body, whose function should only regard sex and the process of reproduction. The contradiction consists in the fact that our soul is ruled by the lunar current, which instead is compelled in the sexual sphere to reproductive ends by the cosmic forces of sound. These, therefore, emerge in us, albeit minimally, as forces of self-consciousness. However, we are not so self-conscious as to perceive within ourselves the force that becomes estranged from us in sex.

In the subtle process of self-consciousness, we can recognize the original forces of sound operating as a power that tends to individualize within us, by means of an activity that is conscious of thought. Therefore, as we have shown, the birth of self-consciousness ends up being connected to a qualitative change of the soul's faculties in function of rediscovering their univocal harmony. The resurrection of human love and of the communion that was proper to the original couple depends on our ability to gather the powers of sound *where they are immanent to us*, not where they become estranged from us so as to operate within us through our subjugation to longing, to fluctuating affectivity and to the forms of sensual pleasure.

In reality, we are cut off from sex, in whose sphere an autonomous process takes place, the consequences of which we are confined to endure—our freedom comprised solely of using forms of bondage at will. We are cut off from sex and in that sense manipulated by it; and, insofar as we are manipulated, (we are) reconnected mentally to it. The impulses of desire hold us by means of the mental (sphere), as this undergoes cerebral processes, in themselves foreign to thinking.

We depend on sex and on a range of instincts, to the extent that our mental consciousness is bound to the organ by means of which it manifests—the brain. This is the limit that consciousness encounters within itself at a given moment. The complex of sensations inherent to sex is transmitted by the sensory nerves to the mental (sphere) bound to the cerebral organ, which is subjected to it without the possibility of mediation. In this way, the spirit bound to the senses becomes longing; and longing, ascending within the vehicle of sensations, becomes thought. *Thought suffers the identity*, because it lacks all autonomy with respect to the sensual content. It is the most humiliating bondage to which we can be subjected, since we assume it as an expression of our very nature or our own right to pleasure. Neither the one assumption nor the other responds to the reality of the human being.

Within our psychosomatic nature, there exist profound errors, or distortions of forces, or contaminations, which wait to be rectified by the *advent of self-consciousness.* They are the consequences of a series of original prevarications, which were essentially the prevarications of sex. Such consequences, taking root in human nature over time, occurred in correspondence to the development of rational consciousness. Today, if a science of the soul arises as an expression of such a breakdown, it certainly cannot offer therapy. Rather, it aggravates the situation. The mission of self-consciousness, as a rectifying force of the breakdown, is the content of Spiritual Science.

The breakdown manifests primarily in the collusion between sex and sentiment. According to a harmonious development of the soul's life, sex would not be able to be felt. What is felt always regards the heart. When feeling lacks the mediation of the heart, it directly affects the cerebral organ and, as such, exerts a destructive action. Just as the eye transmits a content that can arouse a sentiment, but is not what, as a perceptive organ, arouses such a sentiment, so too should the *quantum* of sentiment that constitutes sexual pleasure not be imposed by the meaning of sex, but by its objective content. It should be aroused by the mediation of the heart. But *there is no human feeling capable of such autonomy with respect to the content of eros.* It is what was mentioned in the preceding chapter regarding "platonic love," that is to say, the mediation of feeling required at such a level responds to an experience of the impersonal powers of feeling, possible thanks to the unfolding of a hearing capable of perceiving the metaphysical sound of entities.

The experience—regarding whose methodology we refer to our other studies—corresponds to a stage of the meditative spiritual practice, during which feeling initially acquires independence from willing. One then reconnects with this by means of a deeper accord. The forces that operate in sex need to be perceived as the dynamic life of a transcendent will, to which corresponds the capacity to identify with them in the soul, not according to obtuse sensual pleasure but, rather, according to *an independent feeling*, whose center is the heart.

We have seen how the impediment to human love must be identified in the radical breakdown of sex—a breakdown that refers to the soul's ties to cerebralism, which has become a total constraint at this time, even determining the type of culture. The totality of such constraint today definitively cuts consciousness off from the pure current of feeling, which alone is able to restore to human love its cosmic function, which, in turn, is alone in being able to restore to sex its instrumentality.

Moreover, we have seen how at the level of the greatest inner deafness, self-consciousness draws on an underlying force that involves the reawakening of the spiritual hearing that corresponds to the real life of feeling. The level reached poses the urgent need to receive the forces of Redemption, which operate unperceived within our vital structure, since they have their impediment in reflected consciousness. The sense of the problem can be grasped in the fact that *reflected consciousness impedes the realization of self-consciousness*, even though it is its initial vehicle. The real problem of self-consciousness is being able to perceive the restored original forces.

The perception of such forces corresponds to the reawakening of a capacity of spiritual hearing. For such hearing, these forces can be perceived as sounds, or dynamic resonances, their power being the metaphysical sonority that operated at the heart of the human structure and that of the world. This sound manifested within our physical nature, so that one day we could come to hear it and discover within ourselves the capacity to emanate it and restore our own higher nature. The forces of restoration reach the soul and are assimilated by it, even if initially this soul is unfamiliar with its source—the Event of Golgotha. They are the forces inserted into the Earth by the Redeemer, which, however, only free individuals have the power to realize. The resurrection of spiritual hearing is the undertaking of self-consciousness.

The rediscovery of the primordial sound is a profound intonation within the soul that restores life to hearing, thereby awakening it from a condition of sleep and of death. *It is the sound that reconnects consciousness to the source of the heart*; therefore, it bears *the memory of its original reality* to consciousness—a memory of its kingdom of light, buried in the forgetfulness that has become nature. Forgetfulness is recognized as an area of death that sustains the soul from the depths. It can be defeated by sound that is memory—the memory of a distant good, of a state of truth for which the whole soul is a weaving of nostalgia that emerges in moments of the breakdown of consciousness. It is the memory of a celestial and, yet, human love, music that returns and asks to resonate, as an original manifesting of the soul. It should now express itself because its vehicle is the power that has arisen from its millennial sacrifice—self-consciousness.

Self-consciousness that arises at the cost of losing the original celestial consciousness and the sense of perpetuity can be self-consciousness thanks to the eternal element that nevertheless remains within its depths. Wherever it does not limit itself to being a dialectical perspective of itself, self-consciousness can experience an eternal principle as its foundation. *Celestial hearing*, to which reference has been made, can be considered our perceptive means with regards to the original music of the cosmos. Such an experience, however, leads us to recognize this cosmic resounding within the structure of our organs, in particular within the nervous system.

The nervous system, which from the head to the dorsal spine reproduces the form of the Dragon, is the instrument through which the original music of the universe operated on the human structure. It is *the light's ancient organ of life*, used by the powers of sound to form a being capable of hearing the primordial harmony and to experience it by virtue of an inner vibration. This organ that, according to a meditation given by the Master of the new times, has the form of an ancient stringed instrument, like a *cosmic lyre* used primordially by the powers of sound to edify the human form, ceases to be the vehicle of cosmic harmony when it starts to become an instrument of individual consciousness.

It can be said that the nervous system, originally living as an instrument of the powers of life and of sound, gradually dies to become the organ of sensory and rational consciousness. It becomes a fabric devoid of life, closer to minerality than to organic matter, to provide the mineral experience of the world—the exclusive experience of the senses—to "I" consciousness. Such a loss of the nervous system's original life of light coincides with the experience of sexual necessity and with the beginning of longing's dominance within the human soul.

The need for us to reproduce life according to the schema of sex goes hand in hand with the death of the ancient organ of cosmic sonority, with its becoming (as a neuro-cerebral system) the foundation of consciousness, and with the initial one-dimensional experience of reality—the sensory one—which compels the spirit's current to become the longing for appearance. The original instrument of divine musicality becomes the deadened instrument of sensory life, which, on the one hand, provides us with self-consciousness and rational knowledge—symbolized by the Tree of Knowledge whose fruit Adam and Eve should not have eaten—and on the other, binds us to the animalistic need for sex and to the preponderant series of instincts.

We humans were not ripe for Knowledge. Therefore, having

eaten the fruit of the Tree did not provide us with real Knowledge, but only a *sensory knowledge*, from which there arose the need for the ego, for longing, for instincts, as well as the need for us to lose immortality, so that our cognitive error would not be able to acquire everlasting power. We lose life, which is transferred to our physical body; yet we have no power over the life of this body. We only have the power to destroy it. The body would not die if the "I," with its limited awareness and correlative longing, did not destroy it. This "I," in fact, is conscious by means of the dead nervous system. The deadening of the nervous system results from the loss of life, the corporeal sign of the lost gift of immortality.

By means of the neuro-cerebral system, that is, by means of the deadened organ of reflected consciousness, from which we each draw the sense of self, culture and the content of existence, we are bound to the Earth—not to the living Earth which is invisible to us, but to the Earth as dead minerality. Each form of reflected thought is devoid of life, for which we are compelled to adhere without residues to such earthliness, to identify with it, at its indefinite surface, to *slither* on it—*like a serpent*. Seeing the serpent gives us a sense of disgust and of shame, because it arouses in us an inner, albeit obtuse, perception of our real condition on Earth, of the lowering of awareness to the exclusive life of matter. This identity with matter, in excluding the 'living', cannot but give rise to sickness and to death. After having eaten the fruit put forward by the Serpent, Adam and Eve lose the gift of immortality. If immortality had not been a gift, we humans could not have lost it.

It is a condition of the Serpent for the nervous system to have become an organ devoid of its own life, cold in itself, that receives life from the warm blood of the blood-muscular organism. From the head to the spinal cord, the system assumes the form of the Dragon, namely the symbol of an infernal demonic nature, of a savage egoism, of which human beings can become cured only through suffering, fear, and death. But consciousness bears latent within itself uncontaminated forces of the serpent's organism, namely of the *being of life*, which remains pure in itself, untouched by its degradation. These are the forces of healing, *the true medicine* of the alchemical doctrine—forces that will one day liberate the human being from the necessity of egoism, of suffering, and of death. For this reason, the Serpent symbolizes a degree of initiation.

Through knowledge, we can overcome what the physical organ of consciousness presents to us as a condition of death. We have knowledge, but devoid of life. The reviving of knowledge can give back to us the real perception of ourselves. It can lead us to the reawakening of celestial hearing, necessary for perceiving the secret harmony of the world—*the sound that enchants the Serpent, that of which its being is the deprivation.* The undertaking is the sense of sacred love, namely the impulse by means of which we, by freeing ourselves, shall one day be able to redeem the Serpent. The redemption of Lucifer passes through the liberation of the human being.

Those of us who can discover the life of the light and the warmth of the senses still uncorrupted perceive the movement of the light—the luminous circulation of the blood—which does not need sensual kindling, to have (from the senses) the warmth of light congealed into matter. The cold blood born by the Serpent no longer corrupts. Reviving the life of warmth, there, where it is a pure metaphysical force, we comprehend our own debt toward the serpent—the debt of the lost angelic nature and the abjection of our animal form. The shame of the serpent as an animal regards the human being, not the serpent. If we cease to identify with the sense world, the senses transmit sensory reality to us "uncontaminated by spirit," which, in that case, is not the spirit, but desire. Through the senses, the spirit can rediscover the being that it is.

The level of the serpent, the need to identify with the earth, to slither on the earth, can be overcome by those of us who, through the consciousness available to us, become aware of the level. To this level, we can begin to contrast the level of the sphere in which we intuit the arising of consciousness. We can intuit an even higher level and recognize stages of consciousness that await to be retraced, so that we can realize our true being. Without the restoration of such levels, we cannot realize harmony and love on Earth, which for now we can barely conceive as ideals. The undertaking of the Grail is not only a symbolic reference, but an indicative reality, which, in the background of present human history, stands like the model of a conscious human-cosmic act.

The age of the consciousness soul demands that we discover the lost reality, namely inner perception, spiritual hearing. Inner hearing can restore the true sound to us, the unmistakable music of a supernal birthplace, which was taken from us. We understand that all our human activity, our desires, our struggles, our suffering, is essentially not the longing for what appears, but the desire—profound and unstoppable—to discover the lost place, which can be called an original lost love. All living beings profoundly bear within themselves this willful pursuit, and each time that love with the other being of the couple lights up again within us, we experience, more or less fleetingly, the hope of restoring an unknown good, of which we were deprived. We obscurely feel that in love a path toward lost Paradise opens up, but we do not know that for such a path to be followed it needs to be consecrated. The consecration is the undertaking of the Grail.

The restoration of Eden is the reason for finding this path. It is to hear once again, beyond the soul's lofty regions of silence and of obscurity, the sound of an ancient music, where that of the original beatitude which was lost, returns; at the vision of the beloved's sublime aspect is the dissolution of the human enigma, as the dissolution from the bonds of a long agony.

We must cross a vast field scattered with the dross of shattered loyalty, of destroyed agreements, of the debris of missing donations, of tragic closures in the ego or in the identity with the coils of the serpent. We must pass a field called the *Field of Death*—a symbolic representation of a zone where each human love is shipwrecked, incapable of truly being donated, given that it is incapable of drawing from its own eternal element, even if acting out the attitude of self-giving and of eternity. The Field of Death is overcome by true self-giving, by the love intended for eternity, whose sign is the perception of trans-humanizing music, namely an adamantine reality of the restoration of the other being that, however, is actualized only because this being is ready. It is present on Earth with his or her story, arrived as if at an appointment jointly arranged since the beginning of creation.

To cross the Field of Death means to overcome the easy temptation of renouncing life and the effort that brings about the

Redemption of human existence. It means to understand the gift of life and the mystery that it conceals at the point from which it springs, which is the area of the Tree of Life, whose vision resuscitates the force and the decision of sacred love.

The decisive test is to move beyond the Field of Death, recognizing the illusory nature of all that which seems to stand out as an unavoidable destiny, or as anguish, or as the barrier of human necessity. The test is to recognize the power of death of the original sound's oblivion, because that sound is the memory that guards the meaning of the work and its orientation. Those of us who remember the sound overcome the soul's apparent death. We overcome the danger of believing this death to be true, which is its dependence on the nervous system, truly in a state of death, namely the death to which this (nervous system) subjected itself to serve as an instrument for egoic consciousness. Only by means of such a death could the nervous system help human beings keep, intact, in the lifeless zone of reflected light, in the concept, the virtue of *cold blood*, the open possibility of inner warmth, *independent of the blood's warmth*. The concept's transparent warmth is the slightest initial fruit of so much travail—the possibility of the Logos, which can blossom or can entirely perish.

Those of us who encounter the Logos within the concept have the path toward the Resurrection, that is, toward the possibility of hearing the Logos, *the sound that overcomes death*. The concept right now is the shadow of the Logos, "the shadow of the light"— the life of the light arises within the creative movement of thought, which demands from such a moment the practice of a love that is the life of the Logos. The fact that this life lights up is for us (as spiritual practitioners) a sign that the moment of the re-encounter with the other binomial being has arrived.

The mighty truth flashes to us: "The other is." Wherever we can perceive it as reality beyond the appearance, we see our own Higher "I" come to us from the other (partner). Finally, we discover ourselves. *The Operatio Solis* begins to show us the course of our accomplishment. Where we seek the being of sacred love beyond the figure of feminine grace, we see before us as form, the perennial life of the light, the light that rules the waters, *Stella Maris*. We see as *Marine Light* the *Gateway to Heaven* in its etheric light. The ancient harmony of the superhuman couple, where the original powers of sound and of light merge, is restored.

12.

RESTORATION OF THE TREE OF LIFE

Expulsion from Earthly Paradise, as the human couple's loss of an angelic opportunity, is found in straightforward biblical symbolism. Genesis does not consider the metaphysical and mythical theme that precedes the birth of Adam and of Eve, the theme of Androgyny, or it barely touches it. Yet, in the celestial forbiddance that regards tasting the fruit of the Tree of Knowledge, recognizable is the limitation placed on a state of insufficiency. It is the reason for the couple's corporeal relationship, governed by celestial forces that do not tolerate inadequate human knowledge, or being perceived by an insufficient consciousness with respect to the level of their being.

The waking state of Adam and Eve, despite being a condition of the forces of light, must remain unaware of what occurs in the profound relationship of the bodies. *The nudity of physical bodies is not noticed*, given that the true relationship is between forms of light rather than between bodies. Nevertheless, as such, it is a relationship that implicates a lost power and calls for a ban on access—with knowledge proper at that level—to the mystery of the Powers that continue operating through the division of the couple. It is the work of synthesis that they realized with human cooperation in the Androgyny, symbolized by the other tree of Eden—the Tree of Life, from which the Lord ordered that the couple, having sinned, be held far away so that they would not provide their sinful state with the power of immortality; so that they would not also damage the Tree of Life, which remained intact, and provided the continuity of the human species with immortality, through *eros*, animal reproduction, the succession of birth and death, for which individuals would reincarnate, always having less memory of their own pre-existence, since life would not belong to them. By means of *eros*, they *would long for life, without possessing it.*

The couple's sin was to perceive the corporeal relationship prematurely, with forces of consciousness, not as elevated as those operating within the corporeal structure formed from the separation of the original Androgyny. The separation is reflected in the sexes, but it actually originated from the insufficiency of the light forces of consciousness, with respect to the event of the corporeal part, where the density of the *lower waters,* or of the lunar currents, began to weigh. But indeed, after the separation of the sexes, the Powers of sound and of life, which had supported the androgynous human, were precisely those that could continue their work in the lower part of the body, directing the couple's relationship according to the same Arcane Rule that had made the generation through the separation of the only-begotten human being possible.

For Adam and Eve, to taste the fruit of the Tree of Knowledge was to perceive, by means of an inadequate consciousness, the mysterious process of the union of bodies, as this takes place by virtue of Powers to which a higher consciousness is still not strong enough to open up. Unfolding in such a process is a marriage directed by celestial Hierarchies that seek to continue a divine generation through human beings—a generation that bears within its very structure the capacity to create according to original androgynous impulses that they lost internally. Such impulses continue to act secretly within us. In the gods' design lies the will to maintain, intact, the celestial element of the generation, until the day we humans take it on, to the degree in which we can be consciously correlated with it. Then, the correlation was one of a profound sleep. This capacity of the profound unconsciousness of sex made the couple's *sacred marriage* possible—a marriage that instead would itself also become lost because of a luciferic seduction. For a long time, its restoration *would not even be conceivable* until the original pure impulses operating secretly in the generative process became the inner life of self-consciousness, thanks to a higher possibility brought to the human being by the Sacrifice at Golgotha and by the Mystery of the Resurrection. The human being, as a self-conscious individual, would be free to realize such a life or to reject it.

The cost for us to attain self-consciousness has been the loss of the sacred marriage. The activity of Lucifer within the human soul, sensory vision, the image of the other as corporeality, longing, and the development of rational consciousness are events correlated with one another. Losing the sacredness of the union would cause each member of the couple to lose the other, with whom they were united from the beginning, namely *the only one with whom the original unity could be restored.* Since then, each would seek the other through their bodily appearance—the symbol of a real entity only to the extent that it is supra-sensory. That prostitution, which is the long journey of self-consciousness toward an independence from longing, to which it owes its emergence, would become inevitable for woman as well as for man. This independence momentarily goes through a moment of revolt against the Spirit. Before being able to complete the undertaking of the Grail, Parsifal goes through an obscure and rebellious period. He accuses the Divine of not having helped him in his first encounter with the inhabitants of the Castle. Only when he frees himself also from such dependence, that is, from the submissiveness to a divine power transcendent to him, by rediscovering the Divine within himself, as an impulse toward a heroic action, or as an Impulse of the Christ, can Parsifal re-consecrate the Grail.

That self-consciousness rediscovers the spiritual source in its own immediacy, despite having emerged from an opposition to the spiritual, is the task alluded to in the symbolism of the Grail. The undertaking of the Grail demands to be a conscious fulfillment. In this respect, *it must be indicted as the content of the Initiation of the new times.* It involves a human task that can be recognized as being solicited by the problems and by the catastrophes that the affirmation of self-consciousness opposed to the spirit goes on raising. The theme of Redemption only regards self-consciousness. It is the Redemption that involves rediscovering the correlation of the consciousness soul with the secret of the untouched purity of its vital-physical nature.

The task of the Redemption of self-consciousness and the task of the Resurrection of sacred love are a single task, for the fact that the opposition of self-consciousness to the Spirit is due to the emergence of this self-consciousness from a corporeal constraint imposed by sex. Today self-consciousness can defeat this opposition by overcoming a limit that it has within itself. Overcoming such a limit is more than a cognitive and mental act, in that it is for self-consciousness to unite with its own super-individual source, independent of the vital-physical support. Such an overcoming, unable to be an act of a single moment, but demanding to be continuously renewed by us as experimenters—thanks to a radical self-giving and to an identical will over every obstacle and every re-establishment of mental darkness—is the movement of sacred love. In fact, it awakens to the extent that it finds its own object. As if by the power of destiny, it is led by its inherent transcendent impulse to encounter the being that, through the same movement, has come to the same determination—namely, the restoration of the original accord, so that the spirit does not need the bond to corporeality to penetrate the human being consciously.

A legend concerning the origins illuminates the meaning of the loss of Eden, namely that of Seth's visit to Terrestrial Paradise, when he is sent by his father Adam, near death, to ask the Heavenly Guardians for the oil of compassion. The Archangel Michael permits Seth to enter Paradise and to witness, on several occasions, the region of the over-world. The son of Adam is especially struck by the vision of a big and marvelous tree, in which he recognizes the Tree of Life and the Tree of Knowledge, interwoven and linked together. The Archangel permits Seth to gather three seeds of the fruit of the magical plant and to take them with him to Earth. At the same time, he explains to him the meaning of the new Sacred Tree and of the other symbols of Paradise, giving him advanced notice of the coming of the One who would descend onto Earth to restore the original celestial order—the Savior of humanity. When Adam hears Seth's narration, for the first time since being expelled from Eden, after a long sadness lasting years, he lights up with joy, and he smiles, because he understands that humanity will be saved. Immortality will be restored to human beings, because the Redeemer will come during the last stage of their fall. Human beings will be able to freely decide for themselves about their re-ascent and about their subsequent descent. Within their self-consciousness, this possibility will arise thanks to the supreme act of freedom, which will be founded within humanity by Christ.

Upon Adam's death, Seth places three seeds of the new Tree of Life in his mouth, from which is born a flaming plant. Each time its branches are cut, new branches and flowers sprout from it. From this plant would come the "burning bush." From its wood, the staff of Moses would be made, then the door of the Temple of Solomon, and lastly the Cross of Golgotha.

Human beings would not have lost immortality, had they renounced Knowledge. They would have perennially fed on the fruit of the Tree of Life, had they obeyed the Lord's warning not to feed on the fruit of the Tree of the Knowledge of Good and Evil. Cast out of Eden, they could no longer feed on the fruit of the Tree of Life. Yet, the virtue of such a Tree flows as physical life, corporeal life, *life extraneous to consciousness*, to which, from then on, they were connected through the senses, through longing. Ever since then, the thirst of life, the impossibility of extinguishing it, has been the price that we humans pay for the birth of self-consciousness, the possibility of freedom. *Knowledge is not equal to life*; it lacks the power of life. Life escapes it.

Life and knowledge are separate. But the vision of the two trees fused into one, on which Seth draws during his visit to Paradise as a fateful symbol of the coming of the Redeemer, is significant, since atop that tree, as a culmination of its fructifying, there is a resplendent child, a being just born, a new life. It is therefore the reborn Wood of Life, the Wood forever green, or the Tree forever green, from the golden fruit, which bears within itself the forces of the Sun and of the Moon, the symbol of the magnum opus, or of the androgynous undertaking. Such a vision sums up the meaning of sacred love, or of the undertaking of the Grail. The tree edifies its body by means of carbon, carrying out the adamantine operation that will one day be carried out by the human breath when it ceases to draw life from the air in order to draw it intrinsically out of the ether of the life reawakened within the soul, as the light of reintegrated thought.

In the fusion of the two trees lies the symbol of the adamantine undertaking of sacred love. The two reunite if the duality, consciousness-life, is overcome in the soul, if consciousness finds the power of life, if thinking rises up as living, if consciousness opens up to the heart's ether, if the light's ether within consciousness reunites with the ether of life. Then consciousness is ready to receive the original powers of sound, or of the Word. The Principle of Redemption is ready for the free individual who carries the forces of consciousness to the limit of rationality, to the thresholds of life. *The living*, in fact, *is the true supra-sensory.*

And this is the secret, namely that humans within the sphere of consciousness are able to develop the forces that lead them beyond the threshold of consciousness—the initial movement of sacred love, to which we have alluded in our essay, by expressing ourselves thus: "Only a sacred love rekindled by knowledge, can restore the lost keys of knowledge to the human being."

The "harmony of the spheres"—whose occult symbolism has been considered— is an immanent condition of the Cosmos, and active on Earth. Without the power of the sound ether, life on Earth would not be possible. Neither would thought, nor the human voice be possible, nor the process of reproduction. In truth, the Earth is immersed in the "harmony of the spheres," but the sound of this (harmony) cannot be physically heard. We humans have lost the faculty of hearing such a sound, but we are unaware of our own state of deafness, because from such deafness we draw the awareness of ourselves. The secret of the reintegration is the possibility of listening to the *lost sound*, by virtue of elevating and of intensifying self-consciousness. The *quantum* of blessedness that emerges in the love of the ordinary human couple is the minimal reawakening of the soul's original music. But even this minimal restoration is continuously lost, since it is not perceived, not possessed. Such music can nevertheless be intuited as a profound sense of life and of human relations, where the incorporeal origin of love, its alienation from sex, is understood.

Devoid of music, or of the resonating power of the Word, which are at the foundation of its structure, the Earth is an unreal entity. Human catastrophe must cease to be necessary; death must cease to be necessary, so that this lack of reality can be noticed. Depriving the Earth of its creative sound impedes consciousness from being the real consciousness of the "I." It impedes us from actualizing our true nature.

Human beings would not have been able to lose the immortality of Eden, or earthly immortality, had this not been a gift. We would not have been able to lose it had it been our possession, a good that we made arise and was irradiated by us. The loss of immortality, the "fall," the necessity of sickness and of death, have been necessary for us to recapture as our own being what was merely a gift. Eden is our true kingdom, but it is a kingdom that waits for us to restore it. Such is the sense of the birth of self-consciousness. The Earth's true condition is not the one that appears. The Earth has degraded. All the kingdoms of nature have made the sacrifice of lowering themselves to the sensory sphere. The living has undergone the need for sexual reproduction, to accompany us in experiencing the darkness of matter and to cooperate in the birth of human self-consciousness, not so that this self-consciousness can consecrate the fallen state and arrest itself at a mechanical civilization derived from its embryonic capacity to responsibly rule the Earth. Higher objectives await the conscious human being.

The Earth's condition, which makes material experience possible for us, is temporary. It is not the Earth's reality. All Mysteries and Traditions recall a similar background of the Earth's appearance. This appearance is temporary. It has been necessary for the formation of rational-sensory consciousness, so that this (consciousness) could one day draw the forces to break the enchantment (of the appearance) from the power of its own autonomy. This appearance hides the cosmic reality of the human being behind the enchantment. We cannot fail in such an undertaking, without betraying ourselves, our own nature, our own foundation.

The reality of the Earth is Eden, but the Eden that we can rebuild, insofar as we encounter the presence of the Logos within our will. Even during the period of Earthly Paradise, the Logos was in us, but we were guided by the Logos. The condition for which we are one with the Logos within the inner being of consciousness—where we are free—is different. *We must be free, so that we can realize our identity with the Logos.* For us to have the possibility of freedom, we must initially lose the guidance of the Logos as a transcendence. While we lose this guidance, the Traditions safeguard the memory of the law of the lost relationship. They do not possess the relationship.

In the descending phase, Initiation will always be a reawakening of the transcendence of the lost direction, not the attainment of what will have to come from the consummation of the loss. The completion will be possible when the Logos incarnates within the earthly human being, so as to open up the threshold to the individual element's identity with the transcendence. The "I" will be able to arise as self-consciousness. From this moment the possibility of Initiation will be able to open up, as a fundamental change of consciousness that knows how to preventively reach the point in which the act of freedom, or the pure movement of knowing, coincides with the metaphysical being of the "I." *The Force that once was transcendent to us, becomes immanent to us* in the identity realized—the identity to which the Logos opened the threshold through Death and Resurrection. This is the Resurrection on Earth of the Tree (that is) always Green, namely the Tree of the Sun and the Moon of the alchemical tradition, where light and life are fused, so that the Word can blossom by means of it.

We have seen how the fusion of the two trees symbolizes the adamantine undertaking of the human couple. *It is the great return*, because the drama of the fall begins with the couple's expulsion from Earthly Paradise. Therefore, it cannot but have its ultimate meaning in the human couple's re-ascension. This re-ascension is an event whose initial movement regards the present-day human being, namely the self-conscious human being. It is not an undertaking of the future, but of the present. To the extent that the times are ripe and the birth of self-consciousness on Earth—as we have shown—has no other purpose than that of the rising up of a principle irreducible to lower nature and, therefore, incorruptible, adamantine, capable of confronting what in lower nature opposes the reality of the Spirit.

Our present problems will remain unsolvable if something more than rhetorical or sentimental (if not hypocritical) love, preached by the various social and political morals, does not awaken, namely something living that operates as a power of change of both conceiving and of feeling. In the cosmic course of such change, something already moves within the human being, but it mingles with the recurring needs of the species or of animal nature, as if the new forces did not find in individual consciousness the sufficient purity or impetus, or momentum, or courage that sustain them, so that they are forced to rely on a living element that is only nature, a vital force, a biological impulse. But, as such, they lose their original virtue, even though they achieve a specific capacity to control the terrestrial element on the physical plane.

The vital impulse must not be misleading, because there exists no impulse, no force, no impetuosity on the physical plane that is not metaphysical, or supra-sensory. We have shown how the true force of *eros*, of love, of sex, of willing, does not come from corporality, but from the mystery of an incorporeal principle, of which we are bearers, given that we bear the "I." We have also shown how the reception of this incorporeal principle within us began there, where the conscious will, at the level in which it moves, is capable of an absolute act that corresponds, at that level, to its original reality.

This absolute act is the urgent need of the present moment. It is requested by all people and from all corners of the Earth of those in charge of the spirit. We have been able to examine the terms upon which such an act can today be realized. It must give rise to a transformation of consciousness in the responsible spiritual practitioner, whereby thinking, feeling and willing converge, in the sphere of conscious individuality, towards a harmony that belongs to the super-individual order. Such an order demands an agreement of the soul's three forces within us, to the point in which it begins to compel the lower individual limit. This is the moment of experiencing sacred love, since the force capable of bringing the accord to fulfillment, by keeping intact the pure individual function, is the *dynamis* of the reciprocal correlation of the faculties of both halves of the human couple. The mission of this is what responds to the urgency of the earthly petition. Sacred love becomes *the direct path* of the human being's individual reconnection to the superhuman.

For this reason, *the human couple is one*. This severed union—for which each half (of the couple) tends to rediscover the other through the continuation of the separation and the labored deception of each new experience—exists only for the reconstituted being. The separation is a means. It has been shown how each couple is unique and in that sense *unmistakable*, and how each form of the confusion of (two) halves of the couple ultimately tends toward the restoration of an original accord, without which the realization of the "human state" on Earth is impossible. The human being is an entity in the making that tends toward a fulfillment with respect to which he or she must implement ulterior forces of knowledge. Human beings, in themselves binomial, can realize their original value through an encounter with the binomial being predestined for them from the beginning, since it is the living symbol of their primordial reality. Their path is toward such a possibility. Each couple is unique. Their discovery of one another is the beginning of the restoration of the human to the superhuman—the germ of the re-consecration of terrestrial love.

The couple is one, even when the two do not belong to one another according to the original complementarity. Due to insufficient maturation, the binomial cannot yet be restored. For each of the components, the corresponding binomial half is dis-incarnated and the relationship with him or her continues deep within the supra-sensory sphere, in dreamless sleep consciousness. The existing couple is then the preparer of each person's re-encounter with the other half of the binomial for a subsequent incarnation. Even in such a case, being able to experience the symbol of the oneness, as if it were the definitive one—and only supra-sensory perception can reveal the cosmic background of the relationship—enables each of the two (by means of everyday cooperation and the sacrificial devotion) to prepare the definitive re-encounter with the real half of one's own binomial and to access the path of sacred love. It is evident that, even in this case, the reciprocal fidelity and the sense of the oneness of the relationship are required as a preparatory discipline and as a cathartic introduction to the experience of the soul's forces that will have to express themselves one day in the ultimate encounter.

Once the two components of the original binomial are simultaneously present on Earth, *their encounter has the force of fatality*. It bears within itself the transcendent impulse of a destiny that is tasked with renewing the Earth. The relation of the two, alternately prepared over the millennia throughout the human sphere and non-temporally within the cosmic sphere, expresses itself as a movement of the Earth's regeneration, bringing back to it the Principle of the Light of Life, or the redemptive virtue of the Grail. It is the current of sacred love that has the power to render living, within the human being, the gift of Christ, *which the forces of the past essentially oppose*, the entities binding the human being to sensory appearing, to the illusory game of conventions and of longings, to the darkness of the Earth.

Sacred love has the task of restoring our vision of reality, beyond the rhetoric of semblance, the vision of what is living insofar as it assumes within itself the cosmic, *whose value cannot be determined from below* without being altered. It cannot be determined by the level of the fall, or by the knowledge that responds to a level of the fall but, rather, by the knowledge that recovers the purity of the heights inaccessible to human dialectics, the solitude of the peaks from which flows the stunning breath of the Spirit—the real human level. The restoration of such a level is the mission of sacred love, since it is the only force capable of penetrating into the darkness of human nature without being altered and of reconnecting the movement of life to the warmth of life of the light, so that the separation of the two cosmic currents can be overcome; (so that) the restoring virtue of the One lives again within souls; so that the power of uniting life with what is higher than life may rise again: the power to renew our existence, where death is not needed.

NOTES

1   **Visnuito / Visnuism:** is one of the three main devotional currents (bhakti) of modern Hinduism, together with scivaism and śaktism, which recognizes Vishnu as the supreme deity.

2   **Satchakra sâdhanâ:** an obstacle to spiritual advancement.

3   **Sahasrarachakra:** the seventh chakra or crown center; the **sahasrara chakra** is the center at which one attains liberation

4   **Mûlâdhârachakra: Muladhara** or the root chakra is one of the seven primary **chakras** according to Hindu tantrism. It is symbolized by a lotus with four petals and the color red.

5   **Mâyâshakti:** the power of illusion.

6   **Jîva:** in Hinduism, jiva is a living being, or any entity imbued with a life force.

7   **Albēdo:** the albedo (from the Latin albēdo, "whiteness," from albus, "white") of a surface is the fraction of light or, more generally, of incident solar radiation which is reflected in all directions. In alchemy, it is "One of the four major stages of the magnum opus, involving purification of the prima materia."

8   **Rubedo:** the Latin term rubedo, translatable with "redness," designates in alchemy "the fourth and final stage of the alchemical magnum opus." It is the final fulfillment of the chemical transmutations, which culminate with the creation of the philosopher's stone and the conversion of base metals into gold.